SEEING THE CRAB

*A Memoir of Dying
Before I Do*

Christina Middlebrook

ANCHOR BOOKS
DOUBLEDAY
New York   London   Toronto   Sydney   Auckland

AN ANCHOR BOOK
PUBLISHED BY DOUBLEDAY
a division of Bantam Doubleday Dell Publishing Group, Inc.
1540 Broadway, New York, New York 10036

ANCHOR BOOKS, DOUBLEDAY and the portrayal of an anchor
are trademarks of Doubleday, a division of
Bantam Doubleday Dell Publishing Group, Inc.

Seeing the Crab was originally published in hardcover
by Basic Books, a division of HarperCollins Publishers, Inc.,
in 1996. The Anchor Books edition is published
by arrangement with Basic Books.

Designed by Laura Lindgren

Library of Congress Cataloging-in-Publication Data

Middlebrook, Christina.
Seeing the crab — a memoir of dying before I do
By Christina Middlebrook
   p.   cm.
Originally published: New York: BasicBooks, 1996.
1. Middlebrook, Christina—Health.   2. Breast—Cancer—Patients—
United States—Biography.   I. Title.
RC280.B8M526   1998
362.1'9699449'0092—dc21
   [B]   97-26082
   CIP

ISBN 0-385-48865-3
Copyright © 1996 by Christina Middlebrook
All Rights Reserved
Printed in the United States of America
First Anchor Books Edition: January 1998

1   3   5   7   9   10   8   6   4   2

SEEING THE CRAB

For Jonathan,
by whose presence I learned how to write

CONTENTS

ACKNOWLEDGMENTS

A JOURNEY like the one I describe in this memoir is not possible without constant and loving interest from people on the outside. What writing skill I have is inadequate to convey proper acknowledgment of what the attention of my family, my friends, the members of my cancer support groups, and my medical support staff, both allopathic and holistic, has provided me in this struggle.

I am able, however, to acknowledge how the words of other women who have died of cancer have eased this journey. In particular, I thank Ricki Dienst for telling me, when I was too newly diagnosed to believe it, that witnessing the deaths of other women had taught her that dying wasn't the worst thing in the world. "I figured I could do it" is what she said.

I am also grateful to Pat Connolly, whom I never met, who said when she knew she was dying, "I just wish I had not wasted so much time feeling guilty."

Hearing those words has forever altered how I view my prognosis.

This book would not have come into being without Michael Miller of the *Berkshire Eagle,* who was the first to put this story in print, and Nancy Miller, who let me know that my words did close the gap between the ill and the healthy.

Joy

Joy evaporates
like steam after rain
Rising
from the sidewalks
the deck
the shingles on the house across the street.

I watch it
visible sometimes
as it curls
away from me into the sky.

Other times
the deck is dry,
and the sidewalk
and the roof.
Though the shift from joy
to gone
eludes my eye.

Yesterday,
Driving through the streets
where my children
rode their Big Wheels
skateboards
and mountain bikes,

Memory stirred me to look
and I saw the tail end of joy
as a wisp
disappearing behind the Blues' chimney.

Or,
lying next to my husband,
I remember
the constant and easy
liquid passion
that flooded us
for years and years
and feel my days
parched
without it.

Without joy
It is easier to die.
Easier to leave
this ruined body
which pain has emptied
of fifty years'
laughter, strength and
sheer determination.

Easier
to give up
to slide into the cosmic river
and let my soul

go with the waters,
rush downstream
over rocks and logs
and the discarded tin
and plastic litter
of careless fishermen
and lazy picnickers.

Easier
to reach the mouth
where the ocean looms
with more water
and more force
than I can see across.

Easier,
as joy disappears
with the sun
on the far far other side,
to slip beneath
the surface
of a wave.

February 2, 1995

"I CAN FEEL THIS MORE THAN I WANT TO"

MY HAIR reaches my shoulders now. I didn't think I would live to feel it tickling my skin ever again. The first time my hair came back, it reached only a fuzzy Afro stage before I had to start chemotherapy again. This hair that tickles my shoulders now, this new hair, is about ten months old. My bone marrow transplant was fifteen months ago, and its chemotherapy curl hangs below my ears. Though I look funny, curly on the bottom and straight on top, I am reluctant to cut off the chemo-curls. My hair is decades softer now, like baby hair. They taught me, in the transplant unit, to think of myself as having been born on February 1, 1993. That is the day they poured my peripheral stem cells back into me, to bring me back to life. But the new hair is gray, as well as soft. Truly, I am older, decades older, than I was before.

I need my markers, which prove that something has happened to me. My empty chest is one—I will not reconstruct my amputated breast, though I can never forget how I lost it.

In the beginning, of course, I assumed I'd have the woman-friendly choice: a mastectomy or a lumpectomy with radiation. I had heard about that choice as a major advance in breast cancer treatment. I didn't know, as I believe the world does not know, about the virulence of premenopausal breast cancer. I didn't understand the intentional vagaries of the words *early detection,* which imply that finding a potentially lethal disease early is the same as discovering its cause and curing it. The words that apply to premenopausal breast cancer, words like *dense mammograms* and *chemically induced menopause,* I understand now, don't even fit in the same sentence as *early detection.* We, whose cancers have been diagnosed in our thirties and forties, are always compared to the postmenopausal crowd, those for whom mammograms are accurate and who have already faced the issue of living without estrogen. Truth is, we don't even exercise in the same jailyard.

"Oh God, no, don't worry about the breast." Jonathan, my husband, and I were adamant as my surgeon's words *invasive carcinoma* bounced like overripe tomatoes off the hospital walls and splattered us blood-red with fear. "Take it off. Forget about saving her/my breast."

Days later, as the mastectomy for which I had begged approached, I sat in my bathtub weeping over the loss of that invaded breast. My right breast was purple and swollen from the excision biopsy that had altered the course of my life. It was bruised like the breasts of Argentine women tortured by electric shock, sliced as though a lunatic, confusing sex with mayhem, had assaulted me in a dark alley.

I bade my sick, cancerous breast and my former life farewell. "Thank you for making me beautiful," I told that maimed and purple breast, remembering how it first had appeared, like a pink apple blossom, on my tomboy chest. "You have graced my life with fragile pleasure. My children are healthy and well nourished because of you."

I had only an inkling of what lay in wait in this body then. I think I still hoped that my lymph nodes would be clear. Of course I thought I was in the running for a cure. I had also thought my biopsy would be routine. Jonathan cannot forget how I parted from him, joking a little too much, in a mandatory wheelchair.

"See you in a half-hour," I called to him as they wheeled me away. Hours later he saw me again, unconscious on a gurney.

He asked what they had found. What did a cancer like mine mean? How long would I live?

Then he heard the answer. "She has a fifty percent chance of surviving two years."

I sat on the toilet in the bathroom, head in hands, weeping.

I do need my markers. My empty chest is one. Chemo-curl is the other.

I've been through a lot, fighting this disease. I need the proof, my war wounds, my badges of honor. In the beginning, reeling from the shock, when I felt drowned in information that threatened to swamp all of life as I had known it, even then I said I had to get to know this cancer, this vile crab, and make it part of who I am.

Jonathan is a professor of literature. He is known for his near-perfect recall of eighteenth- and nineteenth-century writers, and also for his misquotes. I had known him only a few months when he paraphrased the theologist, Jonathan Edwards, telling me that "we hang as by a spider's thread over a fiery pit." I, a Jungian analyst, respond to that image. Jungians are determined to acknowledge the shadowy side of life. I have a colleague who consulted once in a nursery school where the children were having considerable nightmares. When she discovered that the teachers (and parents, at the teachers' suggestion) were editing out the evil characters and frightening endings from the fairy tales and nursery rhymes that they read aloud, my colleague told them to stop.

"Read these classics as they were written," she instructed. "Don't interfere with myths that have endured for centuries."

The children's nightmares subsided.

Jonathan and I run a family that believes more in Halloween than in Easter. On Halloween nights past, neighborhood children, eager to trade trick-or-treat candy for admission, have lined the sidewalk outside our San Francisco home. A homemade Haunted House lay in wait on the other side of the garage door that leads to our creepy basement. Truth is, the basement has been haunted far more often than on Halloween. The furnace spreads like an octopus. The dark, covered alleyway that parallels the house is narrow and lowery, filled with cobwebs, dust, lumber scraps, full and empty garbage pails. Pipes hang low and bang the head of anyone over five and a half feet. A decapitated doll on a line seems to fly into the space between the laundry tubs. There are plenty of paint cans and bicycle skeletons to trip over.

Now our haunted basement fills like a tidal pool, mirroring the ebb and flow of our children whose lives, since the diagnosis of my cancer, have moved in and out of this household like winter rains, welcomed after the summer's drought as they freshen each leaf in the garden but apt to leave puddles near the washing machine. The basement is filled with the sacred debris of our lives' time: tents, a Coleman lantern, foam sleeping pads, the cooking pots for vacations at Salmon Lake, skis, boots, poles, tires, obsolete phonographs, a three-legged table, even a pickling vat.

Jonathan has waged a three-year war against the leak from the southwest corner of the garden, cementing, patching, laying plastic under more cement. He is also the beast of burden to carloads, shipments, pickup-truckfuls of foster furniture. We've had the full inventory from my daughter-in-law's apartment after my son came back to marry her and move her to the East Coast. That lot was relegated to the garage part of the basement, because the back part was already claimed by a stepdaughter. Her cartons, each carefully lettered, came in on a wave from high school and college graduations, from an apartment in New York. The wave retreated, temporarily, to digs in Berkeley, but we expect it back when she leaves for a year in Spain.

Another son decided to live in London after graduating from college. His bed and couch are behind the furnace. Half his computer stuff is here, along with mattresses and cartons with labels like "kitchen stuff" and "quilt from Caroline" (his stepmother). The other half of the computer stuff went off to college with his younger sister. I have filled the Secret Room—so called because it was the only place to store Christmas presents before Christmas Eve—with pots and pans and chairs and pillows and pictures and an old rug and a toaster oven and flatware and roller skates that she may want *next* year when she moves out of the dorm to share a house.

What is left will go to my younger stepdaughter. We live daily with these ghostly castoffs, never daring to throw anything away. During my illness our children's lives have maintained a youthful pace, and the basement is still haunted. A skull and crossbones remains chalked on the inside of the alley door. The cobwebs are real.

Jungians believe in integrating evil. We think that if you turn your back on evil, it will sneak up from behind and get you. I have never whitewashed the skull and crossbones off the alley door.

A dear, pure friend, who ate no fat, who jogged while in chemotherapy, who went to an acupuncturist and a Chinese herbalist, my dear friend who told me that cancer was behind her, died. So did Jacqueline Kennedy.

Me? I have a "spot on my spine." In fact, three spots on my spine. "Spot," I have learned, is camouflage for the stink words: tumor, metastasis, recurrence, progression of disease, Stage IV, inevitably fatal— words and phrases you can't say without holding your nose. It took me a while to understand what my doctors were refraining from telling me, as though the knowledge itself were evil.

In an analytic practice, one runs across stories. A young woman arranges for her mastectomy while her children are away at summer camp, then remains firm in her conviction that her son and daughter do not know that their mother is missing a breast. "Cancer!" a certain type of patient may exclaim, feeling outraged and ashamed by her own diagnosis. "I've never known anyone with cancer!" Yet history reveals that a close relative, her own mother perhaps, died of cancer when the patient herself was "too little to understand." This information, which seems so obvious, remains buried for decades. Families have not told. Children, following suit, have not asked.

A friend says that, because of a prosthesis, no one ever thinks about her mother-in-law's mastectomy.

("Except your mother-in-law," I think to myself, picturing my own empty chest in the mirror. "What do you think your mother-in-law thinks when she gets dressed each morning?")

Every morning I look at the scar on my chest where my breast used to be, every evening, every time I shower or bathe, go swimming, put on a bra, take off a bra, decide not to wear a bra. I would like not to notice, I would like not to remember, but I do.

I cannot forget walking, fully alert and unmedicated, into that stark operating room. I can see the stainless steel table where I would soon lie inert, useless and messy like a discarded cafeteria tray, abandoned until the menial housekeeping staff would clean me up. The nurse offered me a little stepping stool, but I was so wired I boosted myself right up onto the table. The flimsy hospital gown fell open at the front. The room was cold. I shivered and no one cared.

"Please," I say, flat on my back, wide awake beneath the eye of a stainless steel Cyclops whose stare shines into my face. "Give me something," I plead with the white coats clustered behind my head.

"Just a minute," the anesthesiologist says as though I were a child whining in the backseat of the family car. "We're setting things up." We'll be there soon. Shut up.

My every nerve throbs with dread. I desperately do not want to cry in front of this harsh parental voice.

The impatient anesthesiologist inserts an IV line in my left elbow. Why haven't I been brought here doped up on a gurney? Why was I told to walk on my own two feet into this operating room as nonchalantly as if I were entering a shop from the street? Do you fix watches here? Change tires? Cut off breasts?

I close my eyes, waiting for the promised anesthesia, fighting off terror, trying but failing to achieve a meditative state. Panic threatens to send me, shrieking, back out on the street and into oncoming traffic.

Other voices come into the room. I recognize my surgeon's. She is complaining about someone who has usurped her parking place. "Where's Ken?" I hear her ask.

"Coming," a voice answers. "Some dingaling has taken the reserved parking."

"I know," yet another voice commiserates.

"Are you ready?" I hear my surgeon ask. "Let's go."

The cut of her scalpel slices across my breast.

The muscles around my larynx strain to speak. "No! Wait!" I try to scream. No sound emerges. The anesthesia dripping into my elbow has begun to paralyze me but has not yet put me to sleep. I can think and hear and feel but I cannot move.

"Stop! I can feel this more than I should!" The words crouch like sprinters poised at the starting blocks. I cannot fire the gun. I try to stick out my tongue, to groan, anything to call attention to my pain. But the cutting continues, sharp and painful, as my surgeon begins to amputate my breast.

My new life begins then, and the vision of my own

death appears. The surgery continues. The pain is excruciating.

Finally the words make noise, like croaks. "I can feel this more than I want to."

Someone says, "What?"

The words come from a distant world, but I can speak. When I try to lift my head, I can. I open my eyes, close them again. "I hurt," that embattled voice says.

"Yes," the someone says. "Lie back. Don't fight. You are in the recovery room."

The gruff, old troll inside me speaks again, from way beneath the bridge. "I'm feeling this more than I want to."

"I'll give you a painkiller."

A squirt of morphine courses through my IV. The mastectomy is over. I am in recovery. They will help me with my pain. I stop trying to speak. But morphine cannot dull what I know.

Denial is the great tsunami. Anger, suffering, jealousy, envy, fear—all are invisible far out at sea. They ride, unbidden, behind the great wave. Then, unexpectedly, denial approaches the shore, approaches where we *really* live. The tsunami crashes, destroying all the pretty structures at the water's edge, disrupting the daily chores, the summer sunshine, the pretense of calm. Denial creeps back to sea, retreating with a mere remnant of wave. Anger, suffering, the clear view of mortality, the knowledge of death, loss, grief—all these clutter the shore like the bleached remains of crabs and clams. We cannot find denial again.

I've combed these beaches since I was young, since the day I learned that my father had committed suicide. I was twenty years old, living overseas, when I deciphered the telegram that said "died" and meant "killed himself." Now my children surround the age that I was then. Sophie, my younger stepdaughter was fifteen when I was diagnosed. Her sister, Leah, was twenty-four. My own three, Ethan, James, and Maggie, were twenty-three, twenty-one, and sixteen.

As a family we disdain codes and are sometimes considered blunt in our truth telling. Also, we are accustomed to storms, having survived a few together. What blew in with my marriage to Jonathan on New Year's Eve in 1985 were his two daughters, who are half sisters, my three children, and on the periphery (because of their presence in the children's lives), his two ex-wives and my ex-husband, who has contributed two baby half sisters. The storms have included terrific passions, fights over custody, and fights over money. Mean letters have come into Jonathan's office. Predawn telephone calls tell us what bad parents we are. With the children, we've weathered squalls about drugs, alcohol, car accidents, unemployment, and which household they preferred. These storms seem, from my perspective now, to have been mere disturbances, tremors that rattled the house to prepare us for the Big One.

At night Jonathan holds me, pulling me in to the

harbor of his body. To my ear he quotes from *Walden*: "Be it life or death," he whispers, the familiarity of his breath as kind as sea air, "we crave only reality. If we are really dying let us hear the rattle in our throats and feel cold in the extremities; if we are alive, let us go about our business."

"It is this," I quote him back, from *The Diary of a Zen Nun*, "as long as I am living I will live. When I am dying, I will die." Today I am alive.

Next there were the phone calls, the giving out of information before we knew what information there was to give. In August 1991, the children were all on the move: Sophie back in Delaware visiting her mother, Leah coming home from New York City, Ethan beginning medical school in Albany, James on vacation with his girlfriend. Only sixteen-year-old Maggie was at home, standing in my kitchen in tears, living the news each day.

I didn't want to break the bad news to my elderly mother, so I left messages for my brother and sister first. They did not call back. Both explained, independently, that they had assumed that Jonathan was just calling to speak of my upcoming fiftieth birthday. This is my family-of-origin's logic. Eventually Jonathan told my mother, who did call back, often. I wasn't answering the phone much.

In 1993 I participated in a research study about the possible genetic component in breast cancer. Questions about my daughter (whose paternal grandmother also had breast cancer) were easy to answer. Not so about my sister.

"I haven't heard much from my sister," I told the interviewer.

"That is surprisingly common," she told me.

It is? I thought everyone else's family rode the tide right in to the bedside. Perhaps not.

There must be a dozen different techniques developed for handling a confrontation with the crab. Should I have kept my diagnosis secret? Should I have worn a wig and carried on as though nothing had happened? My mother, living outside Chicago where I grew up, says *cancer* in a hushed voice. Her eyes roll upward, she flutters her eyelids. I can remember the look on her face when she told me, twenty years ago, that our neighbor had (her voice drops, eyes shift) *cancer.*

Do Jonathan and I talk too much? Were the children old enough to grapple with this news? How old does one need to be to reach into the tidal pool and grab a crab with a bare hand? I know the primordial fear the sight of those claws, the sound of the word, elicits.

I am different from my mother. My children's father taught me how to crab before I married him. He taught me to be aware of the tide so that at the exact moment of its flow, when the pools are low but filling, you can coax a crab from its hiding place. I picture the Earth tilting to pour the water onto the shore, then tilting back again, life washing out over each rock. I see the seashore, the moon.

In time, I taught my children. We caught crabs using smashed mussel for bait. There is a moment when the crab appears, drawn by the scent, a moment when it skitters across the bottom of the tidal pool. You have to go for it right then, without hesitation. Just grab. Pin its belly to a rock, slip your thumb and forefinger underneath its rear end, and pick it up. When the crab begins its feed, that's the moment. It is a moment of faith. Faith that the hold you've taken will keep the wildly swinging claws out of reach. Trust that the claws cannot reach backward to your fingers, or if they can, that the pinch will be just that, a pinch. You find you can withstand the quick pain of a crab-claw pinch.

We would pull off the legs and impale the crab bodies on fishhooks. We hoped crab bait would bring in flounder, sea bass, bluefish. We caught tautog. No one wants to eat tautog.

The crab is a shifty beast, its eyes attached to its body like headlights. Like cancer, it never takes the direct path, preferring to move sideways and furtively. You learn to crab in your own way and in your own sweet time. There may be lots of other people around, a veritable picnic of crabbers swinging buckets and making an oblivious racket. When the moment comes, you pick and choose. It matters a lot who else is there. You surround yourself with anyone you love, everyone you love, friend father mother sister brother wife or husband. You bring someone with you who won't make fun, or belittle, or discount the fear. The children used to require that I sit quietly beside them as the tide came in.

"Cancer has robbed us," Jonathan once sobbed, pulling me over to his side of the bed, "of twenty years." We were married only six years when cancer sidled into our life.

Nine of the fourteen lymph nodes removed from my underarm were positive. Four were already in gross metastasis. When my surgeon brought that news, which came while I was lying in a hospital bed surrounded by flowers and reading lymphectomy/mastectomy pamphlets, the intolerable memory of having my breast cut off dove underground. ("Your blood pressure is low," that dreadful anesthesiologist later explained. "I kept you light.")

Within two weeks I would be absorbing chemotherapy into every cell. My breast would not be mentioned again. Even the subject of a prosthesis did not arise until I joined a breast cancer support group six months later, and the women there told me how and where to shop for one.

My son Ethan is cautious. He hates not knowing. When I first told him my biopsy report, he quoted statistics about early detections. I think Ethan's journey, as my oldest, has been a lonely one. What fate that he would move across the country the weekend after my biopsy but before my first pathology report. He never wanted to go crabbing with a crowd. Never wanted cousins or brother to catch him off guard. Ethan began medical school the week that I was learning how unlaughable was the phrase "funny spot on your spine."

James, my second oldest, in New York when my horrible news reached him, screamed louder than a flock of gulls, calling all attention to himself.

"The news keeps getting worse and worse," Leah said, brave enough not to edit the ogres from this nightmare.

Sophie, at her mother's, whispered, "Explain it to me again, Dad." A voice so quiet as to make no ripple on the water. "I don't get it, Dad."

Maggie stood in the kitchen, her green eyes like pools.

Jonathan managed it all. He made each call, caught all the tears, made all the wearisome explanations. I hardly noticed, so wrapped was I in my own worry. He shielded me until I could find my own ground. I was so appalled at what my body was doing to us all.

Then, each one, in his or her own way, found the courage to reach for that shifty creature and pin it down. Cancer. Our mom, my wife, has cancer. I have cancer. The claws flail. Those side eyes, taillights on a shell, dart back and forth, daring us.

Daring us to go about our business.

2

NEEDLES

FOR US positive-lymph-node, nasty-tumor, forget-about-early-detection guys, oncologists were beginning, in 1991, to add a white blood cell colonizer to the standard killer CAF—Cytoxan, adriamycin, 5-Fluorouracil. With colonizing factor, one could blitz cancer cells with higher doses of chemotherapy in a shorter time, in my case four three-week cycles rather than six.

"Let's hit this tumor hard and early," my first oncologist said, which is why Jonathan and I picked him. "Hit it out of the ball park. Send it into the stratosphere." He talked like that. He'd already given us a consult on the red-flag nature of my pathology report. We were ready to get moving.

Chemotherapy kills all fast-growing cells, not just cancer cells. That's why your hair falls out. But if a colonizing factor has you white-cell-loaded to the max, you can take more chemo in and get more cancer out. At least that's the hope. In a clinical trial run by the pharmaceutical company Sandoz, GM-CSF, the wonder drug, would keep my immune system up so I could handle a 130 percent dose of standard CAF chemotherapy. More and faster sounded good to me, so we signed up. Jonathan learned how to give shots. First we practiced on an orange, then on my thighs.

I had had my first 130 percent dose and was feeling as though my head belonged on another planet. I was sitting in my doctor's crowded office, waiting to have my daily blood draw, when my neighbor and chauffeur, Gretchen, turned to me and said, "Needles! I couldn't go through this because of the needles!"

I looked at her dumbstruck. Gretchen is an escapee from East Germany. Her father, a closet East German capitalist after World War II, wanted his daughter to have a Western education. Gretchen, a young adult in 1961, crossed the border from East to West Berlin illegally every day. Each day she cleverly found a different route to her school so that no attention would be drawn to herself and her nonexistent papers. The Wall went up when she happened to be in the West. She did not go home. In spite of her father's determination that she study in the West, he considered her staying there a betrayal of the family. Between 1961 and 1989, for twenty-eight years, she had no contact with her family of origin. Eventually she moved to San Francisco, across the street from me.

Needles, I wondered. You are worried about needles? At the time of this exchange, my white blood cell count had plummeted. Not even bands, the precursor to mature cells, were visible under a microscope. My chest wound had become so swollen and infected that my surgeon used a large syringe with no anesthetic to drain off the excess fluid. Anesthetics had not worked for me during either my August biopsy or my September mastectomy. By mid-October, I was unable to raise my right arm above my head. I was not worried about needles.

My surgeon and oncologist enjoyed a telephone debate in my presence, arguing about whether or not to rehospitalize me.

This plummet of white cells was predictable. If my blood cells were too quickly destroyed, the daily injections of the colonizing factor, GM-CSF, were meant to boost them.

But I wasn't given GM-CSF. I had the placebo. I was in the necessary control group and had been sticking needles in my thighs every day for nothing. My white blood cells were in free fall.

My recovery required an immediate transfer from the placebo to GM-CSF, and I am pleased to report that this white cell stimulator works. My white blood count bounced upward, as promised. In spite of my allergy to it, in spite of the angry hives that swelled my thighs to grotesque blue lumps, I regarded each new, self-inflicted needle puncture with gratitude. My arm regained its full range of motion.

My blood cells were counted each day during the fall

of 1991, in the doctor's office on weekdays (Gretchen drove me frequently) and in the hospital lab on weekends. Each count required a needle, which, when added to the GM-CSF injection, brought the daily needle count to two. When I had to have dyes injected for a MUGA (to measure cardiac efficiency), or a CT scan, or a bone scan, or on a chemo day, the daily needle count rose. Needles were the good part, indicators of what to do next, to keep me out of danger.

The blue vein inside my left elbow collapsed. The veins in my right arm were off limits to puncturing because, since the lymphectomy that followed my mastectomy, I no longer have a lymph system to carry off infection from my right arm. I wear gloves now (or at least I am supposed to) when I am cooking or gardening to protect me from the little nicks and burns I used not to notice. The medical quest for a place to puncture me was solved by the discovery of a game little inch on the back of my left hand.

"Needles don't hurt," I insisted to Gretchen that day in my doctor's office. My voice had a familiar, imperious tone—like the tone I'd used on a camping trip in the High Sierra a decade ago. Then, the winter past had been a wet one. Snow patches and puddles remained even in August. Jonathan and my younger stepdaughter, Sophie, were plagued by raised, itchy mosquito bites.

"Mosquitoes don't bite me," I announced, with the same animus conviction, staring at the tiny bite marks on my own arms and legs and comparing them to Jonathan's and Sophie's welts. Of course mosquitoes bite me. But I was determined not to pay them any mind.

In January, when the course of enhanced CAF chemotherapy had ended, I went in for my radiation simulation. More needles. Radiation departments are housed below ground (three levels down at my medical center), making it impossible for Jonathan and me to ignore the reality of what they do down there. The rooms are windowless, of course, and burgeoning with state-of-the-art machines.

Jonathan quickly christened Radiation Oncology the "bomb site." I think he expected to run into Enrico Fermi as we stepped out of the elevator. Everyone down there—receptionist, bookkeeper, technicians— smiled and asked "How are you?" We refused to say "fine," but did not discover how else to respond.

Radiation therapy begins with a radiation simulation. They lay me on a horizontal apparatus in a body mold similar to what a podiatrist uses to make an impression of the foot for a shoe insert. In this case, the body mold was to assure the exact same position of my body (me) during the upcoming radiation treatments. They call the body mold a vacuum bag. We started to refer to it as my body bag, as in "What are you going to do with *my* body bag?"

"Don't move anything. Just breathe," the techs told me. So I didn't, for two hours, with my right arm hooked up around my head. Jonathan tells me that their numbers kept coming out wrong and they had to call in the physicist to refigure. Well into the process I told them that my whole lower body had gone to sleep and asked if I could move just my toes. No one responded.

Though I could not see him, I could feel that Jonathan had come to the foot of the apparatus and was massaging the numb stumps on the end of my legs. Slowly he brought my legs and feet back to life. I lay without moving *anything* while the blood tickled and tortured its way back into my veins.

If I were a hostage in Lebanon, I thought, I might have to lie this way for seven years.

"Not too much longer," the tech said. "I'm going to tattoo you now. This might hurt."

She made three superficial pricks around my chest where my breast used to be.

"Hurt!" I laughed, the same scoffing, mosquito-bite tone. "This hurts?"

"Don't move," she said.

Don't laugh.

I cried three days later when I arrived for my first scheduled radiation treatment and they had no record of me. Then, my chin shuddering, I accepted the dare to go about our business. I did the household chores, watered the plants, called to see when I should reappear at Radiation Oncology, thickened my skin against the medical bureaucracy, watched as Jonathan heated up dinner, watched the 5:00 news, answered a letter, took

Benadryl to diminish the welts on my legs, drank milk-shakes laced with egg and protein powder, went to bed, got up, looked at the stack of medical bills and insurance forms. Then, three days and a century later, we arrived for another appointment at the bomb site. This time they remembered my name. Cancer wove its thread through each minute, stringing hours into days, days into weeks. Everything is the same, everything is different.

I signed up to swim at the Recreation Center for the Handicapped, where the water is kept at 94 degrees, and where everyone has one disability or another. My chin wobbled ferociously to hold back tears when the director explained to me that I could not swim laps in the pool during the afternoons because the priority went to elderly people with arthritis.

"We just don't have many people with needs like yours," he said, quite patiently.

Not too many people with cancer, I thought.

Needles don't hurt. Mosquitoes don't bite.

Tattooed for life.

3
THE DRIVER'S LICENSE

M Y DAUGHTER, Maggie, was sixteen when I was diagnosed. She was in the middle of her quest to get her driver's license. As a milestone, a driver's license is deceptively small. In truth it is very big—one of the largest, I think.

"What does it mean, Mom," Maggie asked me, "when I keep dreaming about driving a car?"

"Think about it," I said. "You, in a car."

"Freedom," she smiled, her face lighting up at the idea of her dream. "Control of my own destiny. Adulthood. Getting away."

I had not been eager for any of the children who lived under my roof to get their driver's licenses. Leah, my older stepdaughter, hasn't actually lived here, in spite of her stuff in the basement, and didn't want to learn to drive anyway. The other four—Ethan, James, and Maggie, plus my younger stepdaughter, Sophie— have spent their fifteenth years counting the days until the mythic driver's license would bring access to the family car and all the glorious freedoms listed above. I have not welcomed that prospect: freedom, independence, alcohol, and peril. I have not trusted my sixteen-year-olds to control their wild giggles and/or macho posturing when in a car with like-minded sixteen-year-olds. I have loved them too much to lose them. I want them to grow up. I want to preserve the normal order of things, long life and good health. Parents die first, children later.

During Maggie's sixteenth summer, during those months before my fateful diagnosis, I exhibited the same practiced indifference toward her achievement of a learner's permit that I had shown when her older brothers were at this juncture. "If you're old enough to drive," I lectured, "then you're old enough to get yourself to driving school, old enough to tackle the bureaucracy at the DMV.

"Learning to deal with the outside world," the lecture continues, "is part of becoming an adult. If you can't do that, you aren't ready to drive." For once, the impossible bureaucracy at the DMV was on my side. It and I conspired to make the achievement of a driver's license as chaotic and irritating as possible.

By fall, after Maggie had her learner's permit and had passed driver's training, chemotherapy was making me too sick to drive myself. Maggie was the only child still living at home.

"Do it," I implored her. "Get your license."

"Right, sure, yes. I'm going to."

"Hurry up."

Of course Maggie wanted to drive. Driving meant borrowing the car and not having to endure the hour-long bus ride to her high school. It meant getting home from parties late at night, without having to call me or her stepfather, not having to bicker with us about whether she or we would pay for a taxi if we (early risers—not night people) didn't want to fetch her after 10:00. She never resisted my suggestion that she hurry up with the license. She just never got around to calling the DMV and making the appointment for her test.

On chemotherapy, with my head fogged and my white blood count bouncing around so precipitately that I was traveling constantly to the doctor's office or hospital for a CBC (complete blood count) and platelet count, I needed help. I needed my daughter to go to the grocery store, to pick up the dry cleaning, to take me where I had to go. I also needed to know that she was safe, always.

Maggie was on the junior varsity volleyball team at this high school of hers, one hour away by public transportation. Junior varsity plays its games after the varsity games have finished. Some of her games did not even start until 5:00. Practice did not end until after 5:30. Away games frequently did not finish before 7:00. I couldn't pick her up. Instead I waited, watching the dark descend, watching the clock, holding dinner, listening for her key in the front door, sorry for the hour-long bus ride that prevented her from getting home until nearly 8:00, but relieved that she had made it home safely, one more time. I wasn't using the car. I wanted her to have it, to drive herself. To get home.

We talked about the license all the time. She promised to call to find out which weeknight the DMV stayed open. She'd tell the volleyball coach she couldn't make one practice. She'd try a Saturday morning. Nothing happened.

Discarding my hands-off policy, I called the DMV and made an appointment for her. She was delighted. I was sick and gray and bald, but she could use her learner's permit to drive (with me in the car) to the DMV, and then *legally* drive herself home, leaving *me* to catch the bus, for a change.

She was happy. She told all her friends. She made plans for what she would do with her new freedom.

I remember waiting in the car outside the god-awful DMV, how sick I felt, how I wondered if my baldness and illness were evident underneath the big black beefeater hat I wore every day. During the waiting I got tired. I tipped the seat back to rest, something that Maggie was accustomed to. I had been resting for three months.

She worried that the wait was too long. "We can come another day, Mom," she offered.

"No, we're here. Let's just do it. Let's get it over with."

We waited in a lane named DRIVING TEST. Maggie assessed the competition: only one other teenager, a boy, the kind who looked as if he had spent the last three years under the hood of a clunker he had bought with his own money, the kind of boy who cared more about cars than girls, a shoo-in; then there were some Asian women who could not speak English and a very old man who looked blind. Against these last ones, Maggie thought her chances looked pretty good.

We watched the drill as, one by one, the cars in front of us took on a DMV examiner. Drive forward to the yellow line. Back up in a straight line. Drive out of the DMV lot and turn left across two-way traffic. Maggie thought she could handle that.

We also checked out the examiners.

"Oh, God, Mom. I don't want her. She looks like a bitch."

"He looks nice."

"Geeky."

"Geeky is good."

Finally it was our turn. Maggie got the bitch.

She checked Maggie's papers, still outside the car. "Roll down the window and show me the hand signals," she said.

Maggie looked at me, her eyes suddenly wide. She had gone blank with panic.

I did not turn my head toward her but spoke straight through the windshield without moving my lips. "Hand signals. You know. Stick your hand out the window."

Maggie's left hand shot out the window.

The bitch remained impassive.

Maggie's hand stayed straight out.

The bitch neither moved nor spoke.

Maggie looked at me again.

"Now do the right hand signal," I said, still looking straight through the windshield, teeth still clenched.

Maggie's left arm crooked into a right angle. She looked, hopefully, at the still-impassive examiner.

Nothing.

Maggie looked at me.

Nothing.

"You have shown me two hand signals," the examiner stated. "Are you finished?"

Maggie turned back to me, her face still dumb, stupid, lost.

"*Stop*," I muttered. "You forgot *stop*."

"I don't know *stop*." She sounded as though she were going to cry.

"Down," I said. "Put your hand down."

She did. The bitch nodded.

Then the bitch stuck her head through the window. "You can get out of the car now, madam."

I got out and walked over to a concrete wall to sit down and wait. From there I could watch the old blue station wagon, which we call Blue Lou, go through its paces. I watched Blue Lou lurch (manual transmission) out of the lane marked DRIVING TEST, move forward to the yellow line on the asphalt, then wander dizzily backward. I watched my daughter drive out of the DMV lot, not out the driveway, but over the curb. Then she turned left into oncoming traffic.

"Christina," a crystal voice inside my head addressed me. "Your daughter does not *want* to get a driver's license."

If Maggie got her driver's license and began to drive me to all my doctor's appointments, and to drive herself home from late-afternoon volleyball practices and to the grocery store and to pick up the dry cleaning, rather than taking for granted that Jonathan would do them all, if she pitched in the way we wanted her to, then this fragile shell that I had become, this relic of a mother, would be all the mother she had. She'd be on her own.

Not driving, making me drive despite my chemotherapy, I realized, was her unwitting attempt to keep me alive.

When Blue Lou reappeared, too soon, Maggie pulled it into a parking spot and sat motionless at the wheel. Her examiner spoke to her, briefly, and left. I waited. Eventually Maggie motioned for me to come. By the time I reached the passenger door, she was in tears. She had failed miserably, failed things she knew how to do, driven in ways she had never driven before.

Someone else, it seemed, had taken the test. A wish larger than the one she knew had prevailed.

"You know," I said to her that night, when she was still wracked with humiliation, "we need to talk."

She did not look at me.

"Not about the driver's test. About me. About what is happening."

My sweet daughter paled. I think if she could have evaporated from the room, she would have. I did not dare put my arm around her for fear that she would shove me away and run.

"Talking about my dying, Maggie," I said softly, praying for a stillness between us in which words could be heard, "is not going to kill me. Not talking about it will not save my life."

She melted then and cried. She let me hold her. We rocked together on her bed.

Two weeks later she managed to get to the DMV on her own and pass that hateful test. She also choreographed a dance, for an assignment at school, to the song "Love's Recovery," by the Indigo Girls. The dance begins with two dancers shaking manes of hair like bucking horses. One dancer is weak, the other supports her. They fight and turn their backs. The dance ends with them together again, barely touching, hands at arm's length, but feet moving together in a two-step, a waltz.

4

THE FAUCETS AT O'HARE

M Y RECOLLECTIONS of the beginning are scant.
Summer 1991 was the lump, aspiration, biopsy,
surgery, pathology report, scans, GM-CSF,
chemo. In the fall, the Braves and Twins were in their
last-to-first World Series, and, baseball zealot though I
am, I could not concentrate. I was muddled, too, when I
saw how those weird senators on TV acted toward
Anita Hill. It was easy to think that the Senate Judiciary
Hearings were manufactured not in Washington, D.C.,
but in the confused musings of my chemo-brain.

I was bald as a cue ball, but believed my friends
who told me I looked like a Zen nun, that this new,
hollow look of mine was "striking." I survived by
thinking people might not notice how ill I was.

From the third-floor window of my tall, skinny San
Francisco house, I watched Mr. Zukowski lie in his bed
across the street. Mr. Zukowski was ninety-four years
old. The nurse who tended him was unaware that when

she opened his bedroom curtains, I could look in on him lying, helplessly, sometimes visited by his children but mostly alone, in the blue flicker of a TV screen he didn't watch. Mr. Zukowski was having trouble dying (he had been bedridden for years), and I was having trouble staying alive.

After the senators performed their circus with Clarence and Anita, the Berkeley/Oakland fire blackened the sky. I searched out an East Bay road map and every address book I could find. Sitting at the kitchen table I located the home of every East Bay friend or colleague, people whose kind attentions had sustained me on the new course cancer had dictated for my life. I located the fire's margins, plotted its progress, watched it encroach on some I love. My friends' houses survived, but five students at Maggie's school lost everything they owned save what was left in school lockers over the weekend. I wanted to wrap my dear house around me like a blanket. How could I endure what the cancer therapies were doing to me without my house?

My friend Melissa, a woman in vibrant health, was killed in a helicopter crash.

As the days shortened, as Jonathan drove me to and from the daily blood tests at the doctor's office, I saw that Christmas decorations had appeared. There were eight of us at table for Thanksgiving. At dinner we held hands around the table and I gave my thanks to all five children and their significant others. Jonathan tried to make a toast but wept. The children looked concerned and abashed. A few weeks later, there were nine for Christmas. My family, which had begun with three children, and then, with remarriage, grown to five, is growing exponentially—as if overnight, new partners, serious partners, are included. Some of them have never seen me with hair, did not know me before cancer. Wanting to be good sports, trying to fit in, they joined in by crawling around my bedroom floor, wrapping presents at my feet. I was only slightly aware that this was odd. On Christmas Day, Ethan, my eldest, brought his Nancy to sit on the arm of the couch where I had settled to watch our present-opening ceremonies. He had hoped that I would notice the sparkling diamond that he had given her on Christmas Eve, but I hadn't.

Jonathan and I would be going away for New Year's, the only break I was to have between the months of chemotherapy and the upcoming seven weeks of radiation. Ever since the summer, I had confined myself to my house, to telephone calls and doctors' appointments. Breaking up the constant medical attention was suddenly essential to our humor, so we planned a trip, a gentle trip, to visit Michael and Nancy and find a change of scene.

We had a stopover in Chicago, where the faucets in the rest rooms at O'Hare Airport are activated by an electric eye. One stands in front of the sink in the ladies' room and the eye, sensing life, turns the faucet on. The technology is very advanced. The moment one

moves out of range, the faucet shuts off. On our trip
East on New Year's Day 1992, I stood in front of the
eye and nothing happened. The great stillness I was
living did not carry enough molecular energy to catch
the eye's attention. I had to ask a livelier woman to
come and stand before my sink to make the water run.

Once I would have said that my soul during those
chemotherapy months was as still as death. Needing to
ask the woman at the next sink to stand in for me,
needing to borrow from her vitality simply to wash my
hands, made manifest the fact that I had been separated
from life as others live it. But the stillness of my cells
was most particularly not death.

In January Mr. Zukowski across the street died. No
one opens his bedroom curtains anymore. The fabric
has withered and disintegrated in the morning sun. The
shift from being alive to being dead is absolute. I have
learned that nothing in life can be likened to death.

After failing the faucets at O'Hare on both direc-
tions of our round trip, I returned to San Francisco for
radiation treatment, and the stillness continued. My
bones weakened. My muscles softened. I cried every
day. I felt melted down, myself like water.

At the end of February came my postchemo-
therapy, postradiation scans. These are tests to determine the efficacy of the technology that had stilled me.
All the scans—bone, CT, MRI—are lengthy. My part
was to lie quiet and anonymous while the machines
from Star Wars looked through me. The water of life,

deep inside during the stillness, trickles into the bladder. The bladder fills. A wise move for the cancer patient in these Star Wars drills is to make sure the bladder is empty before the scanning begins.

The department is called Nuclear Medicine and its bathroom is as high tech as its machines. The light bulb in the bathroom ceiling is activated by motion, human motion, within the room. One enters and the light goes on. One leaves, it turns off. When I sat on the toilet, stilled as I was, the light when out. Not having the energy or inclination to wave my arms about, I learned to pee in the dark.

The CT scan showed that my spot, the funny spot on my vertebra, had filled with new bone. "Sclerotic," the radiologist told me.

My oncologist told me I had "beautiful bones."

Jonathan and I took a foolish trip to Paris. We had purchased the airline tickets months before, during a time when we were certain, as the radiology oncologist had assured us, that by March I would be "as good as new." The trip was a gift from Jonathan, to celebrate what we both insisted would be the end of our bout with cancer.

But with computer glitches, which postponed some treatments, and uncalculated holidays, I didn't finish my course of radiation until ten days before we embarked for Charles de Gaulle. Better I had celebrated by staying home and watching the daffodils and tulips come into bloom.

Nevertheless, enough Parisian women wear their hair as short as bristle for me to blend in. And it was refreshing that 8,000 miles away from home, no one knew that I had just finished treatment for cancer. No one knew how lively I had once been compared to how still and gaunt I had become. I remember bits and pieces of the trip, including that my French came back. On our last night we had a happy evening in a bistro near our hotel, explaining to a waiter who spoke no English how to make a Mai Tai. Who on God's earth would drink a Mai Tai in Paris? At the time, the prospect of sweetened rum was soothing. We told the waiter it was a California drink, a comment he took in stride. He was so hospitable that we left a tip in addition to the 15 percent *service compris.* I could understand his appreciative murmur of *d'ailleurs* when he saw it. "Besides." We had left money *besides* the included tip. Understanding *d'ailleurs,* a simple French adverb, gave me an inkling that my brain was returning.

Home again, I found a new pink color had sprouted at the base of my fingernails, shoving the chemo yellow toward the tips. With eyelashes again, I could blink away the debris that had been floating unchallenged into my eyes. I stopped eating bananas, custards, and yogurt milkshakes. One day I stepped up on a chair to reach the pots that hang above my stove. We went to a movie. The children risked getting mad at me for something insignificant.

We took another trip through O'Hare at Easter.

37

Jonathan found me grinning when I came out of the rest room. "What is it?" he asked.

"The faucet turned on," I told him. My body, before the electric eye, was humming enough to make the water flow.

Some things return. Some are changed forever. The animal odors of my mouth, armpits, and crotch, sterilized by chemo, reintroduced themselves. Happily, I found myself needing to do more laundry and making more frequent trips to the dry cleaner. But I still don't know how to dress for a hot day. My choices are to wear my heavy, hot prosthesis in its 1950s sensible-looking bra, or go my old hippie route, braless, and leave my left breast to flop unbalanced and alone. I don't like having to spend so much time thinking about how to dress myself.

Nor do I welcome the knowledge that I will live the remainder of my life in the permanent state of menopause that tamoxifen induces. Sleepless, irritable, drenched with hot flashes. Heavier.

It was hot in Southern California on the June day in 1992 when Ethan and Nancy got married. I danced only the ceremonial dances, with him after he had danced with his bride, with the bride's father, and of course with Jonathan. Ethan was as happy and proud as I have ever seen him.

"I've never danced with you before," I said.

"I know," he answered, holding my body away from his. "It's weird."

The guarded awareness that Ethan's wedding might be the only one of my children's that I will attend gave me the determination to stay up until midnight twice— one night to host the rehearsal dinner, the next to watch Ethan and Nancy drive off in their "Just Married" car with shaving cream on the windshield and cans tied to the bumpers. My whole body ached, I was so tired.

When I had my July Star Wars scanning at Nuclear Medicine, the light stayed on while I peed.

Then I started swimming again. The kind and determined cerebral-palsied, amputees, and paraplegics who use the pool at the Recreation Center for the Handicapped had noticed the months when the fatigue of accumulated radiation treatments kept me away. They welcomed me back and told me that they liked my new, curly hair. Now I have joined an upscale swim club where I undress in a posh locker room with two-breasted women who carefully do not look at my scar. Except for the unpredictable day when I feel too rotten to leave the house, I swim three times a week.

I started reading cookbooks again. Last week, I moved all the furniture to vacuum behind it. I cleaned the dead fish out of my fish tank. I am back at work full-time. Mr. Zukowski and Melissa do none of these things.

5

THE FELLING

―――――――――――― ❧ ――――――――――――

I T SEEMS prudent to have my bone marrow harvested. The odds in favor of my cancer recurring
are frighteningly favorable. I want to have a plan,
such as a bone marrow transplant, in hand should that
nightmare creep in between the daylight hours. The
chief of Hematology Oncology at the hospital that
performs transplants suggests that the spot on my
spine is not funny but suspicious.

"I know," I say, "but what can I do about that?"

"We could biopsy it," he tells us.

No one has ever mentioned that before. I like the
idea. I like facts, hate speculation.

"Chances are we'll get an inconclusive result," he
explains, meaning that a negative biopsy proves only
that there is no malignancy at the exact spot where the
needle hit. A positive biopsy, on the other hand, would
be conclusive. I want the biopsy. I want to know as
much as I can.

This will be my fourth surgery. I carry with me a letter from my surgeon stating that, stoic as I am, anesthesia has not worked for me in previous surgeries. The radiology interventionist, who will biopsy my spine while I am inside the CT scanner, suggests Versed. A good suggestion. During the biopsy I am in a state of bliss, which carries over to the recovery room. I keep telling the nurses to assure Jonathan that I am in no pain.

I am in la-la land. As soon as he is allowed, Jonathan comes to my bedside. I'm feeling just fine. At the foot of my cubicle, where the curtain hangs, I see the hematology oncologist appear.

"It's malignant," he says.

I think, "of course."

Jonathan rises to stand at my feet. The doctor is at my head. Jonathan, I notice, has reached for one of my feet and is holding it.

Something must be wrong, I think. Jonathan is upset.

The doctor spreads my chart, records and reports accumulated over the past fourteen months, over my stomach as I lie there. We have learned to travel nowhere without it. "I don't get it," he says, referring to the other oncologist's comment about my beautiful bones. "If these spots became sclerotic again after chemo, it means they were malignant."

"Obviously," I think.

"Oh, well," he continues. "He didn't have anything more to do for you. I do." He means a bone marrow transplant. Everything seems logical and doable to me.

I just want to get started. The doctor and Jonathan are consulting. I sit up. Their attention swings back to me. I tell them, "It's time to go home and tell the children."

My new doctor winces. I have come to love him for that. "Yeah," he says. "I can only imagine. . . . "

The Felling

The radiology interventionist handed me a chainsaw.
I've been felling trees all week.

My daughter fell softly,
Her green limbs limp around my waist.

"I thought it was over," she said.
"I thought we were finished with cancer."

My sons fell by their natures,
One silently
Alone in a forest without witness,

The other loud,
Unhousing every bird and critter
As he crashed.

Bark, in soft decay around my mother's voice
Crumbled.
"How much money do you need?" she asked.

And then my friends,
Whose sturdy trunks show
Weather
And fire rings interspersed
Among their years,

Could not see the sharp-toothed blade
Unwelcome in my hand.

My news cut sharp
I heard the tall trees
Fall.

Back into radiation. Two more cycles of chemotherapy. I'm going to have a high-dose chemotherapy
peripheral stem cell rescue, commonly referred to as an
autologous bone marrow transplant. Everything I have
so far endured pales by contrast. I am going to do it all
again, but ten times more.

6

CHEATING, OR HOW TO GET READY FOR A BONE MARROW TRANSPLANT

———————— ❧ ————————

M Y CHILDREN say I taught them how to cheat. I did.
Not about taking the boats out on their own. For that I made them swim from the end of the dock to the island and back while I followed, lazy and encouraging, in a canoe. In my memory, I see the determination on their faces and hear their gulps for breath as they roll over to their backs for rest along the way. The water is choppy, and their froggy legs stutter to keep them afloat.

Or about driver's licenses. Jonathan and I argued when that dreadful time arrived. I insisted each learn to drive a stick shift, hills and all. A parking lot near the PX in the Presidio army base near our house has a minimally sloping driveway where three clutches have been sacrificed to my high principles.

Jonathan, for convenience sake, wanted them to take the driving test on an automatic. We fought. I won. So the younger girls failed the test more than once. When Sophie finally did pass and was stuck at the DMV window without both parents present to sign her temporary permit, I taught her how to forge.

"I'll sign for your mother," I said, "and you sign for your father with your left hand."

The children learn, I think, not so much from what I say as from what they watch me do. If there is no cop in sight, no pedestrian in my sightline, I make illegal U-turns. They match my nonchalant stride as we walk by the front desk of our swim club, "forgetting" to have our passes punched when the line is chaotic and the clerks preoccupied. We enter the swimming pool without showering first. Once, when James was in the sixth grade, I helped him concoct a month-long science experiment in one frantic afternoon.

Cheating has been much on my mind since the biopsy of my L-2 vertebra came back positive. I lie in bed thinking of all the reasons why I am an exception to the austere statistics quoted for Stage IV cancer and bone marrow transplants: 65 percent chance of disease progression in three years. Those statistical likelihoods no more apply to me than the WANTED FOR MAIL FRAUD—$250,000 FINE handbills that line the post office walls. I have committed mail fraud, too. For years I sent all my bills stampless, confident that no mailman was going to separate my envelope from all the others headed for Mobil Oil or Wells Fargo Bank just to collect the meager postage due. The mail fraud mega-fine does not apply to me. I have always cheated at solitaire. I prioritize the solitaire games. Won. Won with one cheat. Won with two, three cheats. Lost. Can this upcoming bone marrow transplant fit the same hierarchy? One hundred percent remission. Remission for three years. Maintenance-level chemotherapy. Organ toxicity. Death.

I hate to begin a poker game with nothing in my hand! But I do not fold early. When Maggie was too young to read the cards, she sat on my lap as I played poker. She could not add, but she knew when I slipped a card beneath her butt and switched it when a better one appeared. The idea, I know, was for me to act as though all my cards were good. But I could never master bluffing.

When Jonathan and I play Scrabble, I look at his letters. He, a fine bluffer, will not look at mine, even when, brattily, I turn my tiles around where he can see them. He knows just when to say: "But you always beat me at Scrabble." For a long while I believed him, until I saw the years' accumulation of tally sheets showing that this is not true.

I guess I like to win.

I am intolerant of irrelevant numbers, rules, regulations, statistics, and bureaucracies.

The Solano County dump, long before the AIDS epidemic, refused to accept old mattresses. A regulation to prevent the spread of tuberculosis, we were told. Years ago, when the boys and Jonathan were cleaning out the miserable fixer-upper we had bought as a real estate investment, we had three mattresses to discard. Other folks' old mattresses litter the road into the dump. Some lean into ditches, others molder in the fields. Certain that ours were disease-free, I instructed the boys to hide one mattress per trip beneath the other garbage on the flatbed. Then, past the gate, we tossed them into the bulldozer's path while the dump police were not looking.

A one-week London Underground pass looks the same from week to week. So do the tickets for British Rail. I corrupted Ethan when he was only sixteen years old, on his first trip to England. We had a house outside London and came into town frequently on the commuter train. Feeling awed and foreign, Ethan carefully purchased a second pass when the first week was up. I, figuring to use mine beyond the expiration date, did not. One could look distracted and pass through the gate quite easily.

"But what if he asks for your ticket?" Ethan worried.

To soothe him, I showed him my innocent American tourist face. "You mean the first number is the day and the second one the month? Well, my goodness. We do it just the opposite at home."

Ethan cringed. Fortunately, my ticket was never challenged.

I am not averse to change, though, nor reluctant to

reconsider. In the 1970s, I thought seat belts were a fussy and overprotective waste of time. The cumbersome straps, with their clunking buckles, sank deeper and deeper into the crevice of the backseat while the older children fought and squabbled between them. By the time Maggie and Sophie rode there, just eight years later, I made them buckle up, each time. Common sense does prevail.

In 1991, the first time a hematology oncologist recommended a bone marrow transplant to me, I thought he was overreacting.

"Am I that sick?" I asked.

"No, but you're going to be," he said.

"Asshole," I muttered to Jonathan.

Unable to accept the expert's advice, I pranced off on another route. I got myself into the Sandoz drug company trial, which I hoped would do the trick with less risk. To undergo more seemed too near a dangerous limit. In the late 1980s, before the discovery of white cell colonizing factor and before the development of the technique for harvesting peripheral stem cells, the mortality rate for an autologous bone marrow transplant was 5 percent. By 1993, when my life was on the mat, that grim statistic had begun to fall, which is not to say that my malpractice-wary doctors did not quote the 5 percent mortality rate to me.

"We haven't lost anyone lately," one said, matter-of-factly.

Each of the children has had his or her experiment

with the dangerous limit. Leah left her diary on top of her father's keyboard, open to a vital page. Ethan was in traffic school before his driver's license was two months old. James, underage and with four beers consumed, borrowed a friend's pickup and rolled it through a ditch to land upside down on a neighbor's lawn. Sophie, hanging out at the park before a high school dance, watched her friend Beth consume her first alcoholic drink, a full bottle of Jose Cuervo. Beth threw up in the gutter and attracted the attention of a passing patrol car. We got a call from a police officer at the drunk tank.

"Mr. Middlebrook?"

"Yes."

"We have your daughter in custody."

We answered all these heart-stopping calls, made the requisite phone calls, put on our clothes in the middle of the night. Each time we blessed life that a beloved child was alive to fall apart in tearful, shaking detail at the foot of our bed. When my bad news, that first pathology report, appeared, Jonathan shook too. He nearly dove into my hospital bed with me, lay alongside me, freshly amputated, afraid to touch me in my postsurgery pain, and wept.

"Don't leave me. Don't you dare leave me!"

By January 1993, I am struggling to stay with all of them. Radiation to the lesions on my vertebrae has damaged my esophagus. Chemotherapy, to bring my cancer back into remission, has made me sick and bald again. Christmas pictures show me frail in the corner of the couch for the second year in a row. We drummed at the New Year. Jonathan and I, the children, and a collection of good friends. We warmed up the drums like an orchestra tuning its instruments.

"What is a drumming group?" Ruth's mother had asked before Ruth came over. Ruth explained.

"Oh, you mean like a prayer circle."

Yes, like a prayer circle.

Valerie opens the circle and invokes the gods.

"Whatever comes," she says.

We begin in a circle. Sometimes we're slow to get started. I run my fingernails quietly over the skin of my drum, making a low, scratching sound. John taps with his knuckles. James beats his drum with a drumstick. We aren't looking at each other. Someone picks up a strong, even beat. We follow, quiet, pacing each other. Once the rhythm is established, we play off one another in mixed syncopation, loud and soft. Sometimes Millie sings. Sometimes we dance. I beat my drum and Don's and John's, all three together. I am too weak to dance. Someone makes angry, outraged noises. No! No! We join in, yelling. No! No!

We have gourds and tambourines and rainsticks. We pass the instruments around to share. Because this is the New Year, Nancy and Ethan are here. She tries a flute. Ethan is lost with his head ducked down to his chest, his fingers tapping the ceramic drum. He and Nancy have never drummed before. I pass my drum along and pick up a tambourine. I hear the seeds inside the gourds, rattling against the shell. I am elsewhere, away from cancer, away from pain. Noise, love, and trance-inducing rhythm bounce off my living room walls.

Ruth tells the family to stand in the center. We do, our arms around each other. Nancy, my daughter-in-law, is uncertain about whether to come into the circle. I hold my arms out to her, beckoning. We stand with our arms around each other. In the center, Maggie weeps. I put my arms around her. I pull her head to my shoulder. Our eyes are closed. My drumming circle of friends tip the rainsticks all around us.

Inside each stick, cactus needles fall with the cleansing sound of rain.

The dread, the fear, evaporate. I am loved. I love. I am happy. If drumming is in the running for curing cancer, this drumming will do it. But what is cure, I ask myself? If we have drummed away cancer, what then? Will I live forever? Of course not.

In early January 1993, I begin a daily trek to the bone marrow transplant hospital, which is on the other side of San Francisco Bay. The drive takes a half-hour, each way, every day. First I will have my peripheral stem cells collected. When that is accomplished, I will have two liters of my own bone marrow harvested. The Pheresis Unit, where the necessary blood dialysis occurs, is like a dormitory, three beds on each wall facing each other. Peripheral stem cells are the very first stage of healthy blood cells. Collecting them takes three days if your blood is good but a week if, as in my case, the blood is weakened by a previous course of heavy-duty chemotherapy.

Peripheral stem cells are the treasure. We must collect enough for them to be reinfused in my body after the high-dose chemotherapy has killed every other living cell, which is to say, after high-dose chemotherapy has brought me to the brink of death. The reinfused peripheral stem cells will begin manufacture of my body's crucial new and healthy blood cells. Some bright star of medicine artfully has named this procedure a *rescue*. If the rescue fails, we will rely on transplantation of my harvested bone marrow to bring the good blood cells back.

The force of the pheresis procedure is such that no ordinary little needle, no ordinary catheter, can be used. The machine's centrifugal force, as it spins stem cells out of whole blood, makes a regular catheter collapse. We need a vas-cath. The doctor holds it up for me to see. It looks like a #5 knitting needle, just as thick and just as long. He tells me exactly how he is going to tunnel it into my subclavian vein. He explains why he cannot use an anesthetic during this procedure. I know beyond all knowing that this time I will have to face it straight on.

I lie in the white bed seeing the children's faces, each framed in a time years past. Each beseeches me for one more scheme, one more way to avoid a task that makes no sense. This time I have nothing to offer. The tick of the pheresis machine clicks rhythmically, like a drum. I lie terrified in the sterilized sheets, so still that pain cannot be seen.

"She is very relaxed," the nurse says.

"Very, very good," the doctor responds.

An ache as deep as the breaking of a bone snakes through my chest and down my right arm, withering my will. Oh, to cheat right now. The vas-cath lies buried a knitting needle's length into my chest.

At the end of January, while I am an inpatient kept in reverse isolation, Maggie is going to take a dilapidated remodeled school bus named the Green Tortoise to the Yucatán. Unable to stick around while I face this trial, she seeks her own risk. I promise her that I won't die if she won't. The timing of death is what we scheme around. Do not die now, I tell her, on some godforsaken Mexican highway. Not now, she echoes, in some sterile hospital room.

In the summer of 1992, before the biopsy of L-2, I thought I was well. We went to lots of baseball games at Candlestick Park. The security guard frisked Ethan and Jonathan, my manly companions, probing their backpacks and ice chests like German shepherds after marijuana. Inside my waistband and under my shirt were the family's drinks: Calistoga water, Snapple Iced Tea, Royal Crown Cola. Glass bottles are forbidden at Candlestick because some drunk might throw one at Darryl Strawberry or Lenny Dykstra. We are not the

53

sort to throw bottles. The rules do not apply to us. We hoped the guards would not frisk a middle-aged woman with a radical femme hairdo. They waved me, clinking, through the turnstile.

I dispersed the bottles on the escalator and re-buckled my belt to hold my pants up. I was happy to be alive, to cheat some more, to feel in control, to have outwitted the Grim Reaper for one more day.

7
THE ZOO CREATURE

WHEN ONE is really sick, one can't write about it. During the twenty-five days when I lay in reverse isolation (others could come in, if they were germ-free, but I could not go out), waiting for my peripheral stem cells to rescue me from the near death brought on by lethally high-dose chemotherapy, I was a zoo creature. The puffed face with deadened eyes that I glimpsed by mistake in the mirror belonged in a zoo.

The one door to my room, the entrance to the germ-vacuum chamber where all my visitors disrobed, washed, and robed, had one circular window in the middle. The previous patient had pasted paper fish to it. He told my nurse that he felt like a fish inside an aquarium. I never met this man who had been stuck in the same bed that imprisoned me, but I knew him. He, the fish, prepared the room for me, the zoo creature.

The zoo creature is very dopey. Its left eyelid sags. Its back is covered by a hideous, pussy rash that itches.

The body has no hair, not on its head, its face, arms, legs, underarms, or now-sexless crotch. There is no buffer between it and the world, no hiding. Mammals hide inside their hair. The zoo creature does not know if it is a mammal anymore. Its warm blood is cooled by chemotherapy. It is hairless and no longer able to nurse its young.

The zoo creature cannot swallow. Rabid with thirst, it swishes water through its mouth and spits it out. It vomits buckets of blood. Each blood clot is as big as a baseball, round, and foaming strangely at the seam.

Days later the vomit turns bright green and comes continuously. Retching, retching, retching.

Worst of all, the zoo creature cannot think or remember. It says things in a language that makes no sense. It cannot watch or understand a video, does not read or listen to music. It cannot respond to solicitous messages left on the answering machine. Unable to speak but wanting to make contact, it takes a pen in claw and makes scratches over paper in imitation of human writing. One letter is small, the next too large. The markings wander demented off the page.

It does not know what day it is or whether it is day or night. All it knows is to look to the chair at the side of the bed in hopes that a visitor is there, keeping watch.

8

WITNESS

―――――――――――――――――――――

I<small>T IS DIFFICULT</small> to remember being killed. When I do, my palms sweat, my stomach churns. I feel my voice go sobby. An image from the hospital comes to mind, my flowered L. L. Bean pajamas, and I fling my arms into an exasperated shrug. "Oh, God, it was horrible," I say to block further thought. My mind dives toward the groceries I've just brought in from the car or to a phone call I find I have to make, right now.

The very smell of disinfectant makes me want to leave the room.

I continue, nevertheless, to ask my friends, again and again, what I was like during the days after high-dose chemotherapy had reduced me to a shell. Their anecdotes catch my memory like the stray rosebush prunings that lie in wait for bare feet that walk over our perfect-seeming lawn. I am strangely unsuspecting. Thinking the grass clear of debris, I expect to have a matter-of-fact conversation. I expect the anecdotes to be just incidents recollected at a later date.

One thorn that lay in wait was hidden in a photograph.

Maggie graduated from high school in June 1993, three months after I was released from the hospital. Jonathan shot four rolls of film that day. As is our impatient custom, we took them to the one-hour photo joint the very next morning. We eagerly opened the first packet and saw some man fishing. A photo in the second packet showed a woman in a funny hat looking over a garden of tulips and daffodils.

We were quite annoyed. I hurried back to the photo joint, fretting that our packets would have already been collected by the weird couple on their fishing trip.

"These not yours?" the clerk asked.

"No, these are not mine. I don't know these people."

She frowned, looked at me, looked at the prints.

All white people look alike, I thought, and repeated, "These are not my photos. Mine are of my daughter's graduation, in a gym."

The clerk put aside the first packet, the one with pictures of the man fishing. Those clearly were not mine. Her frown deepened as she fingered through the next, the one with the woman and the garden.

"These not you?" she asked again, offering a print of a bald woman looking out her hospital window.

The pictures of the woman in the funny hat looking at a flower garden were shot, I suddenly realized, from my hospital room when Mary had come to visit. Neither Jonathan, who had taken the pictures, nor I recognized Mary or the makeshift February garden that proliferated outside my hospital window.

I have known Mary for fifteen years. The pots of spring bulbs interspersed amongst the low-maintenance institutional groundcover were there at my request. Before I entered the solitary confinement of my hospital room, I had been consumed with the worry that I would miss the blooming of the fruit trees on my street and of the hundreds of bulbs in my backyard. I had an indeterminate sentence: four to six weeks. I could not bear to miss the spring. But living things can carry funguses and molds, which might have killed me when my immune system was destroyed. Lovingly, my visitors placed pots of flowering bulbs outside my window. From my bed, on the other side of a 7- by 14-feet sheet of Thermopane, I directed them. I wanted the tall ones behind the short, and I wanted the colors to mix. This was my garden, my spring, for the duration. These tulips, daffodils, freesia, hydrangeas, and narcissus comprised the scene I looked at, daily, until I was well enough to go home.

Why didn't I recognize the garden, or Mary, when I saw the photo? Why hadn't the strings of get-well cards hung on the wall, the television looming from the upper-right corner, the swinging arm of the bed table clued me in?

Remembering would be to risk re-entering the experience. If I return to the scene the photograph portrays,

I risk knowing, again, how it felt to have my body obliterated in order to survive. Strange as it sounds, the *I* I was, and perhaps now am again, would not take this risk. That *I* could not take in what the photos showed, just as the same *I* could not absorb the familiarity of the cards and pictures and garden I had used to decorate my hospital room.

Other bone marrow transplant survivors whom I had consulted before I began this ordeal consoled me with startling words. "Don't worry," they said, laughing, "you won't remember a thing. Your husband will, if he wants to, but not you." Could they have been right? What made me so quick to say I did not recognize this place?

On the day I was to be discharged, I sat in a wheelchair on the patio while Jonathan dismantled that garden, so lovingly maintained by family and friends throughout the February storms. He tells me now that he was startled when I said, near the end of my hospital stay, "I hate those fucking flowers!" and that when I got home I was going to burn everything I'd brought to the hospital with me.

My son James arrived that discharge day and was shocked not to find me in bed, my customary place. When he discovered me outside, sitting in a wheelchair and watching Jonathan toss tulips into the trash can, James and I held hands and cried.

"I'm going home, James. You must have left before my message. I'm going home today."

His voice cracked as he took my hand. "You're going home, Mom?"

I nodded.

"You weren't in your room, Mom," he cried. "I couldn't find you."

I understood from his face what he had just imagined. No one was in my room, and half-packed cartons were strewn about. His mother was not in the bed where, on his last visit only five days before, he had waited to empty the barf pans, one after the other, during the constant retching. Following medical protocol so quickly learned, he showed the vile contents to the nurse, then poured the inhuman slop down the toilet, a task no twenty-two-year-old son should have to perform for his mother.

"It was black, Mom, and smelly. Each time I threw one out I thought to myself, 'She is doing it. This is the cancer. This is the evil. She is throwing it up. I can throw it away.'"

I did not remember that he had been there.

He could not know, the morning of my release, that I had just eaten a hard-boiled egg and some bread. His image of me was frozen in illness.

"Did you think that I had died, James?" I asked his frightened face.

He nodded, strangled by tears.

I could feel his torture, the whole family's torture. They had thought that all of me, body *and* soul, was going to die. But *I* had known that if my body had to die, *I* was not going to accompany it.

I had not stayed inside my body to suffer the death of every fast-growing cell. My body was a poisoned wreck: all mucous membranes shed, the inside of my mouth and gastrointestinal tract filled with ulcers, eyelids glued shut with blepharitis. In the mornings I would open my eyes with my fingers. Fevers raged to fight the havoc wrought by high-dose chemotherapy. My urine turned bright red from the bleeding inside.

To save myself, *I,* the me of me, retreated to a far corner above the room. From there, I think, I turned my soul away to contemplate the firmament, to stare at the heavens, the stars and the moon. I found a large psychic cloak and gathered my endangered identity within. Who *I* am could not endure the torture of that room. Without the periodic witness like James or Jonathan, who knew who I was, *I* could not know myself. Not to know oneself is to die.

I know this is the phenomenon of multiple personality disorder and of catatonic states. Abused children, concentration-camp internees, soldiers under bombardment, all may split off from their bodies as I did. With sympathetic witness, I realize now, the condition is not fixed. I was blessed with sympathetic witnesses. I had twenty-four visitors who came regularly to my bedside and, unwittingly, held my identity for me when I dared not. They, my witnesses, chatted together at my bed and engaged in conversations about the world I used to inhabit, as well as about my misery. They waited patiently as I made my weary trips to and from the bathroom, forever wheeling the laden IV pole. They watched me open the mail I could not understand, played my telephone messages back to me, over and over. They watched me sleep my morphine sleep, tried to read the notes I wrote when I could not speak, jumped for the barf pan when the retching began.

But when none of my witnesses was there, I wasn't either. I did not dare stay in the room without them.

I know the day it happened, the moment I retreated to contemplate the firmament from outside that room. My friend John sat at my bedside that day, the second of high-dose chemotherapy.

"I'm beginning not to feel very good," I understated, dizziness and headache assaulting my brain. Suddenly the misery was too much. I can't remember whether John left after that or whether he was still there. I took the person he had come to visit and wrapped her in my arms. My body stayed in the bed, robotlike, to push a call button and get to the bathroom. My soul and *I* departed.

Stuff accumulated in that room. If I concentrate, I can describe it now, though I am astonished at how vigorously my mind avoids the scene. The refrigerator was stuffed with food, cans of juice, Popsicles, yogurt, and ice cream. The nurse told me to save them, in hopes that one day I would eat. Cards hung like laundry on a clothesline. On the first day I had instructed Jonathan how to string them. After three weeks I had accumulated a three-line wash.

In my naive determination, as I prepared for the transplant, I had compiled photo collages of friends and colleagues. I had not finished the job, and the photographs lay in stacks beneath the television. Miscellaneous medical paraphernalia, syringes, and tape, intermingled with hospital brochures, instruction sheets, and my mail, were on a counter. My drum, which I had hung on the wall directly at the foot of my bed, took on an ominous look. In the night the bear in its center bared her teeth at me. The windowsill was stacked with books I had thought I would read. Likewise, audio- and videocassettes remained in racks I had arranged near my bedside table. I taped posters to the doors that locked me in. The walls were festooned with loving messages from friends and colleagues (but nothing from my sister). After that second day, the day *I* picked up and left, they blurred into a Dilaudid haze.

A dietician came to lecture me about following a bacteria-free diet. A kind but uninformed volunteer returned time after time to show me a list of videos and a cart full of library books. I looked at her dully, politely saying "no thank you" until I could no longer speak. Each morning one of the hematology oncologists came to tell me about my blood. Nurses came with bags for my IV pole: the chemicals thiotepa, Cytoxan, and mitoxantrone; platelets and red blood cells to restore what the chemicals had killed off; glucose to feed me; diuretics to reduce the monstrous swelling of my body; unnamed drugs to protect my bladder from the chemical scourge; Xofran and Compazine to combat the constant nausea; Benadryl to clear up hives; Ativan for sleep; morphine and then Dilaudid to diminish the razorlike pain in my ulcerated esophagus and mouth and eyes and eustachian tubes; Antivert for dizziness; Acyclovir to battle herpes and shingles; medicines I can't remember for reasons I could no longer try to understand. I had twenty-six blood transfusions. Each nurse carefully explained the contents of each bag. I learned how to push the blue button for more painkiller. Robotlike, I discussed the dosages. I learned that a bolus is an added burst of painkiller. I learned how to take care of my festering mouth. I washed my gums with sponges five times a day, and gargled baking soda and the antifungal nystatin. Peridex, a disinfectant, turned my teeth yellow.

The staff was diligent in involving me, the me that acted as though *I* were present, in each procedure. They fiddled constantly with the tubes coming out of the triple-lumen catheter in my chest, never once making an injection or extraction without telling me what it was. I bless them for that, not because I could retain what they said, but because their words spoke to their sense that I was human, alive. They were witnesses too.

On the seventh day, after the constant drip of high-dose chemotherapy into my veins, when the white blood cell count had dropped below one hundred and the red cell count was at the bottom, when the hemoglobin and platelets were destroyed, along with my hair, skin, and esophageal lining, technicians brought me my peripheral stem cells. These cells, the earliest initiators of cell growth, had been spun out from my blood during a total blood dialysis process called pheresis. This depleting process had taken place during the weeks before I entered the hospital. Now my own stem cells would rescue me. I remember a strange swishing of ice cubes as they removed the salmon-colored sacks from cold water. Four bags of microscopic stem cells were all that remained of my former self. The hospital guarded this sacred remnant in a refrigerator, just as I guarded, inside my psychic cloak, the tiny spark that is Christina.

Eight days after the stem cell rescue, fifteen days after I entered the fishbowl room, my own blood cells began to regenerate. The body began to fight back.

And why didn't *I* disappear forever during that hideous fight? I think because the witnesses called me back. Not knowing the psychic split that lay beneath the drug-induced stupidities, they treated me as they always had, with love.

Two neighbors from my childhood came from Chicago. They were Ayrie, my childhood bloodsister (we had cut our wrists and crossed them when we were eight years old) and Henrietta, her seventy-eight-year-old mother. In the three days of their visit, we reminisced about the years Ayrie and I spent in and out of each other's houses, about how the doors were never locked so we could walk in and out all summer long. At

Ayrie's house we charred hot dogs over the gas burners and ate them with our fingers. At mine, we were not allowed to play in the living room. In the space between, we made a world with secret codes and elaborate clubs.

During my blood pheresis, another childhood friend, Julie, sat with me. She brought me books and Christmas-card pictures I had sent her of my children over the years. When my body began to shake uncontrollably, Julie climbed into bed with me as though we were still at summer camp. She wanted to keep me warm. My mother, brother, and sister never came to visit, to hold my childhood next to me. After Ayrie returned to Chicago, she persuaded my mother to leave a message on my hospital answering machine. My brother left a message at my house. But Ayrie and Henrietta were there. Julie was there. They knew me. They remembered.

There were other witnesses equally important: a friend standing at the foot of the bed wringing her hands; another sitting near my pillow in the night saying, "Yes, Christina, of course"; someone straightening the stuff around the room; a face bending over mine. They brought me messages from outside, told me stories of my other life. My masseuse came five times to tend the body *I* had abandoned. They asked again and again how I was and listened to the answer. I see them clad in sterilized yellow robes, one so cautious he wore a blue mask.

I moved in and out, sinking and resurfacing. I asked Jonathan when Sophie would come to visit.

"She has already been here," he explained.

From the unhappy expressions on my witnesses' faces, I understood that my words made no sense. *I* apologized. The witnesses soothed me. *I* drifted away. They continued tending me.

Sometimes, when I was alert enough to notice Jonathan's exhaustion, I braved having feelings about him. I fretted about his twice-daily, round-trip commute over the congested Bay Bridge to be with me. Some mornings he was there before I woke. He returned, after work, to stay with me until I fell asleep. He slept in the armchair beneath the television set. I worried that he wasn't eating right. The worry was a vestige of my former self.

I apologized when Maggie, safely returned from the Yucatán, sat next to me during one of my long vomiting stints.

"I'm sorry," I kept repeating. "I'm sorry you have to see me this way."

"Don't worry, Mom," she told me. "I'm not looking at you." Also she spoke words from our other life, the life we'd had before. She wrote how, before cancer, I used to clutch my belly in laughter, not in pain. My daughter remembered that I could laugh. She held my sense of humor, kept it, for me.

Then I came back. It was a Saturday, three weeks after I had gone away. I had not thrown up for thirty hours. The only bag on my IV pole was filled with glucose. The triple-lumen catheter was no longer embedded in my chest. The night nurse came to take my 5:00 A.M. vital signs. I had no fever.

The February morning was still dark. *I* had known the day before that my body was better. *I* sensed it from my place, away, and experimented with the thought. *I* saw that I was sitting up. My stomach had finished its rebellion. I could swallow. Did *I* dare return? My ravaged body was calling for me. Three weeks is a long time to be separated. My soul danced around the shell in the bed, considering. Was it safe yet? Could I?

"I want to go home today," I told the night nurse. "I've been here long enough."

I dressed myself in street clothes, avoiding the sight of myself in the mirror. My mouth ate a hard-boiled egg and tasteless bread. It sipped mint tea. No retching. *I* was ready to pack up the room and flee, but my body was less enthusiastic. Two minutes out of bed and it had to lie down to rest. The weakness was astonishing. But my other part, the soul part, was determined. Now, reunited with my physical self, it demanded that I leave. "Get out!" it ordered me. "Get yourself out of here, quick."

I wept for days after I came home. I called each of the children and cried to them over the phone. I made Leah and James come for dinner. I told Maggie to move back in from her sojourn at her father's house. They sat by me, cautiously, waiting, it seemed, to see if I would break. I was too weak to stand up. Food had no taste. But I was home, in house and body.

The hardest task of recovery has been to tolerate my soul reentering this body that is mine. My heart beats too fast and my skin gets clammy when I think of what happened to my body as *I* was being cured. When I dare, I recall how it looked, lying beneath me. I see my cronelike skull, my bloated torso, my yellow teeth. I feel the itch of the affected skin, the confusion of the constant headache. I cannot swallow. I cannot think.

When we came home, I threw out everything that had been in that room with me.

Now that I realize, by way of the unrecognized photographs, that I made a split during the torture of my body, I am determined to remember more. I want the whole of my life back. I need a continuum from then to now. The experience returns in pieces. Jonathan mentions warm blankets. Leah writes me about my skin. Ethan speaks of the fragility of my voice over the phone.

Mary explains that when she visited, she had the remnants of a head cold and was not permitted to come into my room. Instead, she tells me, she came around to the patio window, where she looked at my bulb garden and threw me kisses through the window. Jonathan photographed us conversing by gesture. Those were the pictures I mistook for those of someone else.

I hear about conversations I had on the telephone. I invited Florence to join me for a cup of tea. I told John I would set an extra place at the table for him. Unless the witness was in the room with me, those events are lost. *I* was not there. I notice that the split occurs still. In the midst of a conversation, I cannot concentrate. Pain lurks. Do I dare feel it? What was I like? What did I say and do? As friends recount, my mind flees to another topic. I have to ask them to repeat.

"You'd leave messages on my answering machine that I couldn't understand because your voice was so frail. I'd really dread coming to the hospital. But when I saw you, I felt better. You were still you."

Sometimes memory comes rushing back. I remember Susan, with whom I have eaten lunch every Tuesday for eight years, sitting at my bedside drinking cappuccino from the hospital cafeteria. I remember Lynn determinedly tracking down aloe vera juice, which I insisted would end my vomiting. (It didn't.) I remember Susan being with me when the nurse came to tell me that my white cells were climbing. Suddenly I can remember a walk I took with Maggie and my IV pole outside the room. My white count had risen to 1,200. My immune system was strong enough for me to enter the hospital corridors. I remember seeing my flowerbed from the corridor window. It was beautiful. I remember a nurse telling me, "Your garden is causing a lot of talk around this place!" Then the tears come and my throat constricts. I am back in the corridor, looking through the window to the patio. I am remembering the wreckage sealed in the room behind the patio window. She is so ugly. She is so sick. When my hematology oncologist asked me, at my first outpatient appointment, whether I would do it again, I was vehement: "no!"

I don't hate the relics of that room anymore. I can think about the things I collected for my stay. I have donated the photographs of all my colleagues to the C. G. Jung Institute of San Francisco. I can read the books, listen to the music, respond to the hundreds of cards, gifts, and letters. I am astonished by the realization that there were dozens of pots of bulbs in the garden outside my window.

Like the lucky soldiers in war, like some physically abused children, some concentration-camp survivors, *I* am still here. We lucky ones who have not gone mad have had witnesses who bore the truth when we could not. I think that's the only way the soul survives.

9

VETS, GRUNTS,
AND ENLISTED MEN

⁂

I SIGN OUT of the hospital on a Saturday morning while my doctor is off for the weekend. He has admonished me that if I go home too early I will be disappointed.

"Monday," he recommends. "I'm sure you will be ready by Monday."

But I can't wait that long. My determination persuades the nurses and the doctor on call. They give me long lectures on mouth care: brush with baking soda, swish and swallow peridex, take nystatin, five times a day. And on diet: no fruit, no vegetables, no uncooked food, no food cooked in public places, nothing that could harbor bacteria. None of their words sink in. I will leave the hospital without nystatin and my tongue will turn yellow overnight.

While they give their discharge pep talk, I begin to think about my house, my bed, my kitchen. I picture

the photographs that hang in my front hall. To my cha-
grin, James and Jonathan have to use a wheelchair to
get me from my room, down the corridor, into the elevator, through the lobby, and out to our car. I am going
home.

The details of my house return to me. Images
crowd in on me that I've not dared to see. I have lived
the last weeks wondering, as I approached each druggy
hospital sleep, whether it would be my last. I have seen
the blur of morning light through gunk-encrusted eyes,
and wondered whether I were still alive. I have not
dared to think of going home. The very thought threatened to provoke deep wails from the bottom of my
lungs. I did not believe I'd ever cross the Bay Bridge
again.

Jonathan drives. The threat of wails subsides. I am
not racked with liberating sobs, as I imagined. Instead,
if I try to speak, my voice goes squeaky with tears. So I
am silent. I feel shy, a misfit, unfamiliar. Did I really live
here once? I ask myself as the city skyline approaches.
Is there a way from here to there? Can I make it back to
the world?

The tears well in my eyes without spilling. I speak,
once. Waving my hand at the never-failing view of San
Francisco Bay, I squeak out one word.

"Look."

"At what?" Jonathan asks.

I cannot answer. My voice is stuck. Home. I am
going home. Home is the sailor, home from the sea.

Home, like a soldier, from the war. Back from Europe, or the Pacific. From Korea. Back to the world from Vietnam. No band. No speech on the tarmac. The modern soldier just goes home and finds the world has gone on without him.

He comes to me often, this soldier, this veteran of injury and war and hell. He comes gently, not waving and grinning—his body is more tentative than that— but smiling. His face is crooked with his own shy smile. He will not speak, I know, because his voice, like mine, is stuck. Our squeaky voices embarrass us. And soldiers do not cry in public. We only cry with other soldiers. We do not risk crying in front of the ones who cannot understand.

The soldier came to me in the spring of 1992, in a graveyard near Bayeux. In France. In Normandy. This was at the end of the first two battles—four rounds of CAF chemotherapy and seven weeks of radiation. Jonathan and I had taken a trip to France to celebrate. We thought our war against cancer was over. We thought we had won.

My soldier has an arched gravestone. I don't remember his name. He was killed two days after D-Day. "We will always remember him smiling," the fading lettering on his gravestone reads, an epithet chosen, I am certain, by his mother. This is the British cemetery on a highway between the town of Bayeux, where the famous tapestry was sewn, and Arromanches, where Churchill, in a fierce storm and under fire, towed the landing docks he had built in England through the high tide off the coast of France. There he secured them so that he could feed and clothe and arm and succor and command his army. The British cemetery—in contrast to the American one over by Colleville-sur-Mer, where crosses and Stars of David make pure white, polished rows—has uneven rows of gravestones, the kind you'd find in a churchyard. Crumbly and individual. Daffodils grace the faces of some. Some are long forgotten. The stones, their lettering, the size of the plots, each is different. Each chosen by a family. Some say "Daddy." Some quote Wordsworth, or Auden, or the King James version of the Bible.

We have toured all of Normandy. Jonathan is such a World War II buff that he has to look at every bunker. Sometimes I go with him in the March air and look out over the sea. Sometimes I wait in the car. I am most comfortable here, in the British cemetery, with the soldiers and the loved ones who commemorate them.

They died so young, you see. They met their fate so early. I am fifty-one years old. Fifty-one and I don't believe in wars ending anymore, or in battles always being waged in a foreign land. There have been so many wounds suffered in my hometown this year, so many battles endured. I am tired. Shell-shocked. I have breathed too much poison gas.

Home from the hospital, I am confined to my bedroom. Foggy-headed. Weak. I dream about the smiling soldier I met in that Bayeux graveyard, dead at Arro-manches. Or I think of him, American this time, at Point du Hoc, a ranger, climbing a cliff in the face of German artillery, climbing against impossible odds, in impossible peril. Perhaps, I think, compared to a twenty-year-old ranger, I have had it easy.

What has happened to me? How can I make sense of it? The technology that has saved me has killed me in order to rescue me. We destroyed villages in Vietnam, too, in order to save them. I remember that. So here I am, destroyed and saved, returned from war, at home injured and recuperating, receiving visitors. I'm back in my own bed. I get to use my own bathroom and look at my own garden. I eat yogurt from my own refrigerator. My loved ones have received me joyously. Yellow-ribboned glory comes with every phone call. Everyone is anxiously waiting for me to pick up life where I left it, eighteen months ago. My mother rejoices that I am home early.

Early. I cannot digest that concept. My night ter-rors, sweats, depressions, fears, none of my shell-shocked reactions have disappeared with "early." Did we get out of Vietnam early? Some say we did. Have we listened to what Vietnam vets finally made us hear about what happened to them after they got back to the world? Post-traumatic stress disorder finally became a legitimate diagnostic category in the 1980s. I remember considering it a novel concept. That was before I became a soldier myself.

These days I'm not diagnosing post-traumatic stress disorder. I'm living it. I don't go out of the house, except to the doctor's office. I wear a sterilized hospital mask. I don't go to the grocery store, or the movies. I don't eat in restaurants. Hell, I don't even eat, yet. Remember the vet who comes home and lies in his bed staring at the ceiling? The one who doesn't even listen to music or read books? Well, I watch an embarrassing amount of daytime TV. I watch *Donahue* and Sally Jessy Raphaël. I am addicted to the 5:00 and 5:30 and 6:00 news. I watch *Hard Copy* and *Cops.* I know every episode of *The Golden Girls.*

Oh, God, what company that traumatized soldier provides me! I keep him inside my pocket like a talisman. I think he understands me. I think I understand him. I think of the graveyards that we have left behind, now that, supposedly, the war is over. I hear the guns far off, raging in the distance—someone else's body now. Paula's, Deborah's, Ricki's, Ann's. But cancer, like war, has fallout, like nuclear fallout, and it suffuses every breath I breathe. I think the soldier lying on his bed, staring at the ceiling, declining to sit at the family dinner table, refusing to go out with his old friends, is, as I am, trying to figure out how to go on with life, trying to figure out whether it is worth going on after the nightmare.

In my ceiling-focused reveries, I wonder whether there was another era, different from this, when the words for illness and war were not so irretrievably intertwined? Can I understand better what has happened to me as I lie beneath and inside the machines of medicine—so advanced that they are equal, I am sure, only to machines of war—can I understand better if I think of war?

Crowded quarters—tanks, submarines. The bone scanner lowers to a mere whisker above my face. Inside the MRI, where machine-gun noise fires into my ears and makes my skull vibrate, the tube in which I lie is no larger than the inside of a torpedo. A voice from the ceiling—Eisenhower? Schwartzkopf?—during my CT scan barks commands—"breathe"; "don't breathe." I comply. They are talking to me, I realize, from the war room, the place where strategy is mapped. They make their plans, scheme their strategies. But *I* fight the war. *I* obey the orders, feel the loneliness and the pain. *I* travel deep inside myself to suffer the indignities, to endure the unspeakable, to dream of my soldier.

He is not a man-soldier, not an officer or a general, but a boy-soldier, an enlisted man, a grunt. Like me, he is scared, brave, and overloaded with gear. He has been handed a minuscule life expectancy but is too exhausted from the struggle to care. He neither sleeps nor eats. He is tired, impatient, but so determined. I feel the determination down to my knees. I never look back. I never consider other options. I just do what I have to do.

What I, what *we*, soldiers and cancer patients, have to do is go it alone. We leave everyone and everything we have known before, discard every plan, change all priorities, and go to join the troops in the chemo-therapy barracks. There the others, the short-timers, middle-timers, new recruits who enlisted just months before we did, all the other people with serious cancer, have made an advance patrol. They know the terrain. We follow them, frightened, daring to trust, utterly dependent on what information the scouts can relay back to us. Poisons drip into our veins. Radiation scars our lungs. Bureaucracy diminishes us. Impersonality enrages us. We are irritable, wet, cold, seasick, vomiting. We are bad company. Shivering. Sulky. Self-centered.

I remember that when I was fighting this war in the pheresis unit, Julie put her arms around me as though I were her child, or as though we lay together under bombardment. She tried to get into bed with me to warm me up. I remember Julie when we were thirteen years old and unhappy. I remember sitting with her on a couch in her basement TV room. She reached out her arm to me and I snuggled up to her. Two lost little kids, alone. And here we were forty years later, on the beach together, one wounded, the other frightened, keeping fear in a far corner of awareness. Not particularly brave. We simply had no choice but to be where we were, and with each other. Buddies.

Bad weather. An unexpected infection. The battle, which is to say the bone marrow transplant, has been postponed. I find no relief in the delay. The soldier inside me is ready, extravagantly ready, to flail down cargo nets into landing craft that promise no safety in a rolling sea. I am insanely ready to run through waves onto a beach while shells and mortar and bullets and grenades burst at my head, and at my face, and kill my friends, and leave a smell that will make me throw up forever.

The ramp has dropped, admission day at last. I charge straight into the sea with water up to my hips and rifle overhead. You can't shoot a rifle when you are holding it over your head. I flail through the hospital corridor, too frightened to feel frightened, and admit myself to the reverse isolation of the transplant unit, where the battle for my life awaits me. Previous chemotherapy is a mere skirmish compared to the major battle I will fight in the transplant unit. By the time the ramp is down and the $35,000 up-front hospital down-payment made, the soldier in me is no longer feisty. Just passive, resigned, beyond thought. I've lost my rifle somewhere and cannot find it.

Jungians might name this boy-soldier of my imagination, who is so crucial to my struggle, a contrasexual figure, my animus. He is my female image of masculinity, vital to my androgyny. I am not a girl-soldier on this beach.

We played boys, my best friend, Ayrie, and I. We grew up together in suburbs that were downright rural compared to what they have become, in a time when children were kicked out of the house on a summer morning and told not to come back until supper time.

In a time when being bored was not a problem an adult wanted to hear about. No one needed to worry about where we were. We didn't particularly care to come home. I remember exactly where we climbed trees, rode bikes, made clubhouses, built forts, dug, swam, and, in the dead of winter, made daring forays into the ice caves on the Lake Michigan beaches near our homes.

We played capture-the-flag and kick-the-can. We rode horses and fell off and got back on. Sometimes the horses trotted under the low limbs of trees to knock us off. Sometimes they ran away with us, and we got in trouble for losing control of them. We rode bareback. We played scout. We imagined being orphans, getting lost, being kidnapped. We wanted to be pioneers. I remember summer camp, where I was initiated into the Ojibways. And as an Ojibway, with Ayrie, we competed with Iroquois (my sister was an Iroquois) and Pottowattomie and Ottawa. We had swimming races and canoe races and sailboat races. We climbed trees and forged rapids and made portages. We built campfires. We fiercely identified as Indians—not squaws, not cowboys. We were braves.

Those brash masculine days are over. The soldier of my fantasy now, the boy-soldier who travels with me in my middle age, has become obedient. He takes it on *faith* that the battle he faces has a higher good, just as I take it on faith that the bone marrow transplant gives me a better chance for life. We have learned, when we reach the promised safety of the beach, that it is not safe. Our task is to inch our way forward. So we do, slowly, continually betrayed by the unexpected. We fight little. Mostly we suffer. We're on Iwo Jima now, waiting. As cancer continues its assault from hiding places neither general nor oncologist know exist; we remain shivering, cold, wet, sick, and always trying our best. Possibly wounded. Certainly frightened. Possibly dying—or already dead.

We think neither of the future nor the past. The boy-soldier just focuses on living one more minute. A curtain has descended on the unknowable future. Unknowable things disappear to another time, what Jungians might call an Ego time. In Ego time, humans have control. I can remember that time, but it is lost to me now. I can remember the illusion of time that my Ego took as real. And I remember the power that human beings think they can harness. I'd name it Ego power. That other power, the one I live with every minute of my new life; that other power, like weather, or plague, or synchronicity, is the real power, and it does not come from the Ego. It comes from what Jungians call the Self. Others call it God. I just think of it as the big stuff. Fantasies about being in control of my own destiny have evaporated like sea smoke.

Sitting in my bedroom waiting for the medically imposed quarantine to lift, waiting for hunger to return, for the ability to swallow more than once at a time, I don't have a thought of the future. Well, I think about the time when Maggie will get home from school, or when Jonathan will call to check in. When my brain can, I remember who is coming to visit, who has been assigned the task of checking up on me. I remember and then forget and then remember again, to ask my neighbor Martha, who checks in on me often, to help me make my bed. I want her to go into the basement and tell me how much rainwater is trickling through the basement floor underneath the washer and dryer. But I am not fretting about winning that battle. I have lost any thought of returning to my old life, watching my children enjoy graduations and find work and marry and have children. I do not think of my work, and its attendant conferences and meetings and committees. There isn't any question anymore about my retirement, that mythological time when I was supposed to have earned enough money and enjoyed enough success to relax. I do not expect to know my grandchildren. I do not expect to grow old. I don't even think about the spring.

Sometimes I'm lost in the jungles of Vietnam. I picture it—not the scream of bombers overhead or the whup-whup of helicopters coming out of nowhere and leaving just as quickly. But as a grunt. I have been vertically inserted into this jungle by wonderfully complicated whirly machines that abandon me once I am on the ground. My boots are wet. My feet have rotted. I am trained to find and annihilate the enemy, though I don't know, really, who the enemy is. I am fighting the heat, the rain, the mosquitoes, the snakes, unidentifiable jungle creatures. Just as on the beaches of Normandy, I fight little, endure much, suffer, wait, and rely on my buddies. Contrary to all my training, training that promised that the more prepared I am the more apt I will be to survive, I learn that training is for nothing. Bombardment. Incoming. Forces of Nature. Those are what may kill me. Nemesis is large, impersonal, random, unfocused. No help my marksmanship, my physical fitness. No help my positive attitude, my willpower, my fat-free diet.

The Ego is no more help in surviving the beaches of Normandy or the jungles of Vietnam than it is in curing Stage IV cancer. Preparedness is irrelevant. Consciousness is irrelevant. What matters is to continue, with all the enduring and long-suffering aspects of the feminine—determination, endurance, obedience, love, patience—which, suddenly, my boy-soldier has assumed. Acceptance and fear of death. These feminine qualities abound, not in the heroic way, not in a blast-your-way-out-of-it Rambo way, but in a waiting-on-the-beach way, a tramping-through-the-jungle way.

The battle rages, the mortars come in, the bombs drop, the boy-soldier, that nonheroic, anonymous boy, and I make do. We've learned about friendly fire, as apt to kill us as the enemy, and we don't really care anymore. We just make do. I love my boy-soldier. I just lie here and think of him. The picture of him soothes me like a warm hospital blanket. Tears of admiration load my debrided, gunky eyes as I imagine him debarking from the landing craft or the helicopter and submitting himself to the possibility of death. I like it that he is so resigned. I like it that he doesn't ask for much. I am astonished at how much younger than I he is.

10

FINGERNAILS

———————— ❧ ————————

My FINGERNAILS and toenails are coming off. So far I have lost the nails from the index and middle fingers of my right hand. After my high-dose chemotherapy bone marrow transplant, the living nails died. Now, ten weeks later, I notice the new healthy nail pushing the carcass of the old one out from the cuticle. The dead nail is yellowish and ragged. When the new one has pushed it about two-thirds of the way toward the quick, it catches on something. Then with a quick tear of pain, it pulls off.

In the Middle East or Bosnia, wouldn't this pass for torture?

Fingernails are handy tools. A person needs them for turning the pages of a book, for opening envelopes, for buttoning buttons. When they are ragged and snaggy, they catch on things: the inside of oven mitts, pantyhose, long sleeves.

It is hard, without fingernails, to collect coins out of

a coin purse, to pick up stray pieces of paper, or to scavenge a paper clip out of a drawer. The metal pour spout on a box of dishwasher detergent is an impossibility.

Without fingernails, when the quicks are newly exposed and tender, tucking blankets under the mattress hurts. I find myself resistant to filing insurance forms simply because I know that fingering through the cardboard folders will hurt.

I am wearing earrings with hooked wires through my pierced ears because I can't get the backs off a pair of studs. Jonathan and Maggie fix the clasp on my necklace, unbutton my tight jeans when I need to pee, remove shrink-wrap from bottle tops.

I've taken to scratching my itches with a table fork.

If this had happened two years ago, I would have screamed and yelled, called the doctor, complained, and worried. Now I wrap the tips of my fingers in Band-Aids and try to get on with my day.

These days of recovery are slow, as slow as the growth of new cells. My hairdresser tells me that hair grows at the rate of half an inch per month. I can't see it happen, but were I to look in the mirror only once a month instead of every day, I could.

I measure my recovery by the space between what I could not do ten weeks ago and what I can do now. Ten weeks ago I was in the hospital and could not swallow. I found a pathetic note I'd written when I could not speak. It said: "The first human instinct is to swallow, and I cannot."

Six or eight weeks ago I could not even get out of the bathtub alone. I was too weak to tie my own shoes. The task of making my bed was so exhausting that I could not do it by myself. A journey down the two flights of stairs to the kitchen was as carefully planned as one abroad: advance notice necessary for a change of plans, minimum/maximum stay required, travel restricted to prearranged hours. My return to the third-floor bedroom was fixed at one per day.

In the hospital I was made to shower twice a day, an elaborate procedure that entailed unhooking me from my IV pole, waterproofing my triple-lumen catheter by plastering scads of tape to my chest, leading me dumb and stumbling to the shower stall, sitting me down on a chair underneath the spray. Two showers daily were required to counteract the thiotepa-induced rash that covered me like acne gone wild.

On my first night home, I lay in a bath scented with vitamin E oil. No IV pole hung over my head, no catheter opened my chest, no water-rotted chair was in the room. But I could not get out of the tub. Normally, I can remember now, one lifts oneself from the tub by clutching the sides and using bicep muscles to bring one's body into a sitting position. The motion is fluid: up, legs folded briefly, feet collected underneath, then a step out of the tub. Everyone does it this way, I guess. I've never needed to think about it until now.

Jonathan pulling me to my feet and steadying me as I stepped out of my first at-home bath was horrible, like an old, old, woman aided by her long-suffering son. His patience these long weeks has humiliated me.

Six weeks ago, I could not taste. My esophagus went into spasm every time I took a sip of water. My doctor warned me about dehydration, but I could not take more than one swallow at a time. I learned that eating was easier than drinking. When I ate, I took a bite, chewed it, then swallowed. When I drank, my thirst wanted many swallows in a row. Impossible.

No fruits, the staff admonished me when they discharged me, no fresh vegetables, no frozen yogurt. Eat well-cooked foods. Drink juice only from cans. Do not let anything that can harbor bacteria through your lips. Do not have people over who have not already visited you in the hospital. Wear a mask whenever you go out, particularly for appointments with your doctor (waiting rooms are filled with sick people).

Do not garden. Do not go into hot tubs. Do not swim in a public pool. No movie theaters. No grocery stores. No circulation in crowds. W. C. Fields said that the only thing he lost when he was on a diet was the will to live. I understand his despair.

Oranges and bananas, because they can be peeled, are safe from bacteria. I craved them. The first banana I ate tasted like cotton batting, the orange like water. What is the point of living, I thought, if I cannot weed my garden, swim, go to a movie, or enjoy my food?

But my new hair follicles were growing. Beneath my cuticles, new fingernails were replacing the old. I rediscovered how to get out of the bathtub. I used the water's buoyancy to lift myself. As the water drained beneath me, I began my first exercise regimen, lifting myself up and down in the water, hands on the edge of the tub, up and down as the water beneath me lowered. The lower the water, the more difficult the lift. Each night I do these water-assisted push-ups. Now I can do ten.

I no longer need to keep track of the trips up and down the stairs.

In the beginning I ate breadsticks and popsicles, cottage cheese and canned pineapple chunks. The taste of sweet returned first. Chocolate in steamed milk. Jam on cream cheese. Then we planned a day, two weeks after my release, for a picnic in the Marin Headlands, a place we could drive to in the car. I anticipated this day with as much excitement as a holiday on a tropical isle. I made the lunch. I covered myself against the effects of the bright spring sun with #15 sunblock, long sleeves, a hat. Jonathan ate a tuna fish sandwich forbidden to me because of chopped-up onion and celery. I had a carton of Yoplait (the sweet taste of strawberry-banana), breadsticks, and a box of pineapple juice (the sweet taste of pineapple). He drank Calistoga water. My esophagus fizzes and burns when I drink anything carbonated.

We spread our blanket on a ridge overlooking Fort Cronkite and the Pacific Ocean. The vista was too beautiful. I was frightened outside of my cocoon. Jonathan wanted to hike farther. While he was gone, I waited on the blanket, wondering what would happen to me if something happened to him.

During those first weeks home, I did not want him to know that I did not want him to touch me. I needed him near me all the time, but my body was too erratic and unpredictable for touch. My internal thermometer had gone haywire. Most of the time I was insufferably cold, wrapping myself in silk underwear, turtlenecks, and wool sweaters. I kept the oven on so that I could open its door and let heated air in under my sweater—a colonial housewife lifting her skirts in front of the cooking fire. I could not get warm outside of my electric blanket, even when the spring warmth sent the outside temperature to 76 degrees. Then hot flashes returned, sending steam through every pore, plaguing sleep.

My only refuge was the bed, where I wanted to lie, undisturbed, to lose myself in the meaningless prattle of daytime TV. Or I would leave the front door unlocked and lie listening for the footstep of one of the select group of caretakers who came regularly to check on me. I waited for the sound of Maggie returning from school. I talked on the telephone. I watched my garden, watched the rain, so impatient, waiting for strength to return.

One day I picked up a glass of water and took six swallows in a row.

Then I discovered that playing simple pieces on the piano, things that Mozart wrote before he was ten years old, helped my brain. I could feel it grind into motion, feel the momentum of improved thinking as I concentrated to coordinate the fingering of the right hand with the left.

Ten push-ups from the bathtub. Two twenty-minute practices at the piano. Of course, I must put the piano playing on hold now for the molting of my fingernails. But I am not tortured by this latest delay. Tiny things are happening. I can taste my food. I can write letters. Jonathan orchestrates a simple dinner party for my aunt and uncle, dear to me for their attentiveness. My brother comes to visit, and we go to a restaurant. When he and Jonathan order drinks, I order chamomile tea. The waitress says "sure."

I plant herb seeds in sterilized soil and place them in the western window of my bedroom. Basil sprouts faster than coriander. My fingernails shed faster than my toenails.

The migration of my dead nails fascinates me. That, the spring, taste, increase in muscle tone, a sexy dream about Jonathan, all mark my progress. As the new pink nail emerges, I clip the edges of the old one, noticing how slowly and surely it lets go my flesh, distancing me from the day when all my healthy cells sacrificed themselves so that all the fast-growing cancer cells might die.

11

SAILING

~

I AM AT the tiller. The gusty Lake Tahoe winds bat at the mainsail, first from the starboard side, then from port. Jonathan is being patient and I am swearing. We are trying to bring a rented 14-foot Laser II back into the harbor. The wind is capricious and offshore.

Our butts are bruised from landing on strangely placed deck cleats, our fifty-year-old knees sorely tested in the tiny cockpit. We have just spent four hours climbing over each other, tangling in multicolored nylon lines, giving each other instructions, comparing anecdotes from thirty years ago when we each used to go sailing.

A Laser II, we are learning, is designed for one person, a racing person. That we are not racing people is evident each time we come about and the sails flap sloppily while we try to get our bodies arranged. Jonathan names the cleats these sleek sailboats have nowadays, cleats that catch the main and jib sheets and hold them for you, "snatch blocks." We are having a wonderful time.

When he speaks of snatch blocks, Jonathan fixes the jib sheet in one so his right hand is free to pat my thigh. People tell me that I look good these days. I find it disconcerting. Shortly before we came up here, I found myself in conversation with the pleasant-looking man, perhaps a little younger than I, who shares a waiting room with me before our appointments with our analysts.

He told me (his first words to me after months of waiting together without looking at each other), "You are really looking good."

This comment might have stirred my hormones two years ago. Now I am visited by self-consciousness. I respond "thank you," my voice shy as a six-year-old's.

"The change," he continues, "is really quite remarkable."

I check out the cover on the latest *New Yorker*. "It's been a rough go," I speak to a William Hamilton cartoon.

"I'll bet it has," he smiles, kindly. "Congratulations."

"Thank you" is all I can think to say, again.

This man obviously has understood why I have looked so ravaged over the past year. His words to me are sensitive, but I am humiliated. I still cannot imagine how sick I looked while they were trying to cure me. Now that the treatment is over, and we have no idea what my prognosis is, people think that I am well. Most do not follow my metaphor when I speak of the unpredictable Lake Tahoe winds.

"You're a miracle," they say.

"An inspiration to us all."

I hear this every day, just because the gray and shaky effects of my cancer therapy have dissipated. The treatment, which turned me into a Holocaust victim, is confused with the illness, which, at the point I am now, has no visible symptoms. I look well. I have survived a bone marrow transplant.

"How *are* you?" I am asked, many times a day.

Should I give an answer about my blood counts (still below normal), about how thoroughly my body has changed? My sleeplessness? Hot flashes? About the spasm in my jaw that for weeks has prevented me from closing my mouth? I bruise so easily that my fingers turn blue from simply taking off my rings. My feet hurt, lots, all the time.

Should I tell them how much time Jonathan and I spend debating whether it is advisable for me to submit to all the scans (CT, MRI, bone) and blood tests that will tell us, before we need to know, that the devil lurks within? Or should I smile and tell them how well I feel now, how I can swim thirty laps and have gained fifteen pounds?

I don't *know* how I am.

On Lake Tahoe we sail from calm to gust and back again. During the calm I fiddle with the tiller and mainsheet, trying to coax some speed from the slightest ruffle. "Just where is this wind coming from?" I mutter. Then, from nowhere, the wind picks up and the Laser tips, menacingly, into a steep heel. I panic. Rather than riding the crest, enjoying the speed I've sought, I grab the mainsheet from the snatch block and release the tiller. The Laser obliges by sashaying directly into the wind and returning to an even keel.

I had thought I'd lost all fear.

Everyone asks me and my family if the bone marrow transplant was "successful." They want to know if the cancer is gone, if "they got it all." Often, they cannot hear the answer when we give it. The answer is that a distant metastasis always recurs. Recurrence is inevitably fatal. The bone marrow transplant has prolonged my life, prolonged the treatment-free time, not saved me. My family and I live daily with the (more than remote) possibility that I am dying.

"Geez, I'm sorry," I tell Jonathan, embarrassed at my own panic. "It'll take me a while to get used to this."

We had fantasized sailing as in the old days, with water rushing over the leeward rail and ourselves hiking out to windward. I think I have lost my nerve.

"This is the first time I've seen you more frightened of something than I," Jonathan remarks.

He is speaking not only of the chemotherapy, radiation, three unanesthetized surgeries (including the mastectomy), and bone marrow transplant, but of Class V rapids, downhill skiing, scuba diving. I introduced him to each. He damn near died running the Caldera on the

Upper Klamath River. He went out at the top of this Class V rapid and "swam" it, as they say. He tells me of a calm moment under water when his wrist was momentarily caught between two rocks. "Oh, shit, I'm dead," he thought in the second before he worked his hand free. I remember watching him at the mercy of white water, terrified when, at the bottom where the river stilled, I saw him floating on his back. I thought he had broken his back. He tells me that he was collecting his thoughts.

Voluntary risk taking has been our idea of fun.

Now, sailing, I am startled by his words. Has he *never* seen me more frightened than he? Has he forgotten the great Loma Prieta earthquake of 1989, when I sat immobilized at Candlestick Park, watching the seats above right field bob and weave, slanting perilously into a heel the way the Laser does now? On that day, Jonathan laughed and went for a beer, guessing the quake at 3.2 on the Richter when it was actually 7.1. I stayed in my seat, heart pounding, hands trembling so violently I had to put them in my pockets to still them.

And what about the dive at Playa del Carmen, when he and James wiggled like eels into a narrow cave to visit a nurse shark? I waited at their feet, my heart pounding uncontrollably, my breaths coming so fast that I thought I'd suck all the air out of my tank.

The same happens now, when I think we are going to capsize. My heart is like a Tom and Jerry cartoon, pulsing from my chest like a respirator sack. Despite the inner commotion, I seem unable to move. At Candle-

stick Park I did not think to get out from under the concrete overhang that might have fallen on my head. On
Lake Tahoe, I freeze as I watch the water rush closer to
the cockpit, the foot of the mainsail dip near the waves.

Preparing for death is as inefficient as preparing for
what we in San Francisco have come to call "the next
Big One." We mean the earthquake that will bring the
city to its knees. Though we all know how to turn off
our gas lines and strap our hot-water heaters to the
wall, how to shore up our foundations and teach our
schoolchildren to "duck and cover," the truth is we
won't be ready. But we try.

Recently, in my own preparation, I talked to a
mutual friend of my ex-husband and me about how my
children might manage with him as the lone surviving
parent. "Oh, you don't really think that's going to
happen, do you?" she was quick to reassure me, thus
depriving me of any information she might have had
about my children's future. "You didn't go through all
that bone marrow misery for nothing. You are going to
be just fine."

The subject changed, and knowledge of my foreseeable death slid away—from her, not from me.

I don't think it ever slips away from me.

I am terrified of capsizing.

Cancer will kill me. It will sneak up on me, make
microscopic but lethal invasions into tiny parts of my
body without my even knowing it. And while it happens, I will be looking healthy.

In another conversation, Maggie and I are driving home with an old friend after having watched the performance of a play James wrote, performed at an undergraduate playwright festival, about a son going crazy when his mother is dying. James is vehement that the play is about him, which it is, and not me. It is also about his old girlfriend, Tiffany.

Tiffany, James's father and stepmother, Maggie, my old friend Linda, and I sat in the same section of the theater, hugging one another and crying a lot, much to the annoyance of the rest of the audience.

When the final bows were over and the lights came on, Linda said, "Wow, James. You sure write good fiction."

Tiffany, her face bloated with tears, added, "Yeah, not a word of truth in it."

On the way home, Linda asks Maggie, matter-of-factly, whether Maggie thinks it easier to have warning of her mother's death than to be hit unexpectedly, like our friend Amy, whose mother froze to death during a school field trip on Mt. Hood. Amy was twelve years old at the time.

Maggie is quick to answer, and I agree with her, that having time, having warning, is better.

We like at least the illusion of control.

My wish is to sail the Laser on a close haul directly toward the beach. From the middle of the lake, this seems plausible. As we approach shore, however, the wind disappears. For a moment the mainsail sways out at a right angle as though we were running free. Then a ripple in the water indicates that the wind comes now from port.

I had thought I'd tack as close-hauled as possible into the offshore wind. If things were predictable, a deft coming-about would put us on a broad reach parallel to the shore toward our mooring. This wind is not predictable. Just fifty yards from the harbor, after another teasing calm that I've endured with my sails so tight as to put the boom right in the cockpit with us, the devil wind picks up speed and slams us from the stern. The Laser bolts forward. The slack mainsail comes to life with the force of it. I am too panicked to grab the mainsheet out of the snatch block.

We scramble to the high side. I cannot breathe as I watch the leeward deck submerge. The Laser, bound up in too-tight sails, careens over, slowly. The tip of the boom snags under the water, all in slow motion. Water begins to pour into the cockpit. I have lost control.

But the water feels wonderfully cool. I grab my hat and watch Jonathan's head sink below the surface. Then we are treading water, with the skitterish mainsail now like soggy plastic under water. Behind me the hull rolls over slowly. An instinct, thirty years dormant, disentangles me from the sails and lines. The Laser is dead in the water, the mast pointed to the bottom of Lake Tahoe, daggerboard protruding insignificantly erect from its belly.

With Jonathan's weight on the daggerboard to roll the hull and my memory (I remember to release the mainsail from the vacuum that keeps it just beneath the surface), we bring the Laser back to life. The tall mast lurches upright. Teenagers in a powerboat have been circling, offering help, which we refuse. They cheer and speed away as the mast heaves out of the water.

We appear to be doing well. No one from the powerboat looks back over his shoulder to check our progress. They must think that having the Laser upright is cure enough. But when Jonathan tries to heft himself back into the cockpit, the Laser rolls 180 degrees again. I don't know how we will manage with no help.

Obviously, to keep the Laser from rolling over again, *I* must clamber back on board first. Jonathan must remain in the water on the far side and hold the boat level. Am I strong enough? It is impossible for him to lift me in as he used to lift me out of the bathtub when I first came home from the hospital.

My first effort to lift myself is a miserable failure. I cannot get the center of my weight over the coaming. Anxious now, adrenaline coursing through my veins, I wait in the water, collecting my energy. "You have to do this, Christina," I admonish myself.

Placing my hands on the deck as though it were the side of a swimming pool, I summon all my strength. With a wave buoying my life jacket, I heave myself up. The life jacket catches the coaming and refuses to move. Panting with exertion, I reach for the daggerboard well and pull. Suddenly everything gives. I, like the great mast and sail rolling upright, whoosh over the deck into the cockpit.

Now that I am back on board, it is easy for Jonathan to join me. We sprawl in the cockpit like two upended beetles in life jackets. The boom sways overhead.

"You all right?" he asks.

I am just grinning. I flex my biceps, beat my chest, stoked by having just pulled my full body weight up out of the lake and back into this boat.

"Can you believe it? Can you believe I've ever been sick?" I ask him.

"I can forget it," he laughs.

That night an inexplicable light rises from behind the mountains on the east side of the Tahoe basin. We are sitting on Don and Valerie's deck finishing dinner as daylight changes to night. A gray thunderstorm has just passed by like a locomotive. Jonathan and I have tested the hospitality of our hosts by insisting that we remain outside on the deck with its fabulous view. I am an invalid again, wrapped in extra blankets to keep warm as the temperature drops. They are sharing a bottle of wine. My esophagus is still too raw for alcohol.

Don thinks that the eerie light must be the unfortunate effect of light pollution, the urban lights of Carson City now so strong as to blot out the starlight. Jonathan states that something is seriously wrong: the now-brilliant yellow light reflecting off the bottoms of the thunderclouds is light from an A-bomb test in the Nevada desert. I say that it is the Second Coming.

The light grows more and more brilliant.

"This is it, you guys," Valerie says. "Judgment Day."

Then the full moon, as fat, natural, and large as all time, slips over the top of the snow-capped range and ascends into the thick clouds above.

No disaster, just the moon performing its cyclic miracle one more time.

The next day Jonathan and I take out the Laser for another sail. We rig the sails ourselves and generally congratulate ourselves on our increased skill. But I insist that Jonathan take the tiller when we begin the complicated tacking back to our mooring.

The wind is as tricky as ever. Once more I watch the foot of the mainsail dip under the waves, watch white water surge into the cockpit. In the exact same place, the very spot where we capsized the day before, the wind switches force and direction. It happens more quickly this time. Jonathan loses control, swears "oh, shit, not again," just the way he did when they lost track of my records in radiation oncology for the second time. We plunge into the water with the Laser wrapped around us. Soon the mainsail is trapped beneath the surface of the water, the hull has rolled belly up, just like the day before. This time I am not afraid. The maneuver to right ourselves is routine.

We can get used to this.

12

CURSING GOD

———— ❧ ————

M Y BLOOD counts are in a slump. The hematology oncologist explains how there is a lull in cell manufacture after the work of my transplanted peripheral stem cells subsides and before the work of my own bone marrow takes over. I wonder if this explains why my hair and fingernails have stopped growing again. I haven't needed to shave my legs for months, and a chemo line is creeping up my fingernails again. My spirits plummet with my white count. I'm tearful, frightened, and without stamina. No one can do or say anything right.

"You look well," a friend remarks.

"Hmmph," I snort in response. What is well? I certainly don't feel well. I just feel alienated.

To divert myself from how uncharitably I am behaving, I focus on the pennant trauma of the San Francisco Giants who, like me, have lost their summer's zest. If the Giants can hang on, they'll meet the

Philadelphia Phillies in the National League Championship Series.

As children, my sister and I were Chicago Cubs fans, childishly fervent in our support of a rotten team. Now my loyalties are in San Francisco and my sister's are in Philadelphia, where she lives. The irony that these two teams might meet for the final battle when she has not contacted me voluntarily since Ethan's wedding in June 1992, not even after the confirmation of my metastasis/recurrence or during the bone marrow transplant, is not lost on me. Normally I would have called her, not to place bets but to commiserate. As former Cubs fans, we share an innate lack of faith in the adopted teams of our adulthood. I don't really expect the Giants to win the pennant. She doesn't truly believe in the Phillies. At least this is what I imagine. My sister's absence from my life during this phase of my cancer ordeal has been curious and painful.

Then she calls, on the last day of the 1993 baseball season. The Giants are about to hand the National League pennant to the Atlanta Braves. My sister says something about baseball.

I cannot respond. A lot has happened to me in the fifteen months since we last spoke. For all I have thought of her these past months and felt her silence, for all that, it takes a moment for me to recognize her voice. Christmas, a year ago, Jonathan extorted a letter from her. "If there is anything you want to say to your sister," he chided her, "anything from your shared years together, *now* is the time to say it."

She wrote that she felt helpless to know what to do. She said that she thought about me every day and that she loved me. I wrote back immediately: "That is what to do. Tell me that you think about me. I don't believe anyone in the family has ever told me that she loved me."

My plea for her attentions, for increased expression of the affection we automatically have for each other, did not work. I didn't hear from her again until this phone call. Her voice is there, unannounced in sisterly familiarity. She knows I know her. The recognition comes like nasty ground balls. "I can't believe this!" I sputter. "I can't believe that you're calling to talk baseball. In all I've been through this year, I haven't heard a word from you."

"I'm sorry. . . "

The two-year, maybe forty-nine-year, batting slump of things unsaid is over. Disappointment and yearning ricochet off the ivied walls. "I almost died last winter!"

"I didn't know that."

"What do you mean, you didn't know?"

"Mother said you were doing well. That you got out of the hospital early."

I got out of the hospital after twenty-five days instead of twenty-eight. How many days, how much suffering, warrant the comment that I am *not* doing well?

"I don't understand!" I wail to her. "The only reason I would ignore someone who was having a bone marrow transplant for advanced breast cancer would be if I didn't care, or if I didn't like her, or if I was really mad about something!"

"It's not that," my sister weeps. "We're just like that. It's not personal. Mother and I . . . "

"*You* might be like that, but I'm not. I don't care if that's the way the family is. *I* don't want to be that way. You are the only sister I have. We could be there for each other. We could be like other people," and then, just to be mean, I recite the names of all the people I know and my sister knows who have reached out to me with cards and phone calls and money, each name highlighting her absence.

I yell at her for everything, for ignoring our father's death, for being an absent aunt to my children, for bringing her children all the way from Philadelphia to Los Angeles for Ethan's wedding and then treating the weekend as though it were a chance for them to go to the beach rather than a chance for us to be together, for continuing the arch coldness of our family.

"I don't want you to treat me the way we treated Daddy." My words come unbidden. "I remember how we treated Grama when she was dying, and Nin. I remember our uncle. I don't want to be treated this way!"

When they were dying, they were alone in scattered Midwestern convalescent homes. I made just one short visit each to Nin, my beloved nanny, to our uncle, my

mother's brother (both of whom had lived with us in Chicago while I was growing up), and to Grama, my father's mother. I don't think my mother visited them much. There was no family precedent. We talked about them, but our words never made their way to them. This is our family way.

I prefer my sister-in-law's way. Judy stood on the balcony of her condominium when her husband lay in the hospital dying from prostate cancer, and shook her fist at the sky. "Fuck you!" she yelled. "Fuck you, God!"

I think that only those who believe in Him curse God. If the name of God is passion, fury, or vitality, if God is the very stuff of life, its dailiness as well as its nightliness, its love and hatred and intimacy and joy, its force and inertia, its knowable and unknowable spirit, then mine is a godless family. And a godless family does not curse God at the death of its daughter or sister.

Memory: I am very, very pregnant. Within hours of Mother's arrival, I head for the hospital to have my third child. My boys, then four and six, are out. When they return, Mother, confident of her own decorum, carefully does not tell them where I have gone. She deprives herself of the experience of their childish reactions. The boys have been awaiting the birth of this new sibling (to be named Steve Austin, they announce, if he is a boy, or Maple if she is a girl) with four- and six-year-old curiosity. My mother finds my delight in bringing the new child home too showy. She tells me that I make too much of things.

"Not too many toasts," my sister would instruct me about Ethan's rehearsal dinner, seventeen years later. "About four toasts would be right." To my great pleasure, James played master of ceremonies and coaxed nineteen humorous and personal statements from friends and family.

"Did you think there were too many toasts?" I asked my sister in the warm afterglow of the dinner.

"No," she conceded. "I thought it might go that direction, but it was fine."

There is nothing in my family's godlessness, no clue, no yearning, no instinct, nothing that enables them to share with me the inevitability of my early death. For years I took this to be their indifference. I have felt much criticized and often disliked. I see it now as fear and envy, as misguided self-protection. They will not cope with their own ends any better than they have the rest of ours.

My father killed himself on New Year's Day 1962, when I was twenty years old. I was living in Edinburgh, and in the scant correspondence between me and my family at the time, no one suggested, though our family always had enough money for such things, that I fly home to Chicago for his funeral. The focus, and I was party to this at that time, was on whether or not his death (accidental, we hoped the world would believe) would be mentioned in the newspaper.

"The funeral wasn't too bad," my sister wrote me. "The minister only mentioned his name once."

Then and now, we do not mention our father among ourselves. But I can imagine him drunk and weepy in my hospital room, making trouble with the nurses, calling attention to himself, consumed with loving agony. He would have telephoned often. This I know, because he called me often in the year before he died. His calls were sobbing and sentimental, slushy with alcohol. I used to get so mad at him. "Oh, go have another whiskey," I remember muttering before I was old enough to know the difference between scotch and vodka.

"What?" he'd demand. "Speak up."

"Have another whiskey, Dad."

"It's not worth a damn, sugar. Not worth a damn."

I know he would have carried on as much for me as he did after his father's death, when he wept for months. Were he alive, Daddy might have taken a plane to my hospital bedside, providing me with the security of being irked by his familiar, drunken ways.

I see him, massaging his shoulder as he often did, talking about a book he thinks I should have read, dropping names, attempting wit. His mouth is soft and he carries a bottle of vodka concealed in his briefcase. I was well grown before I realized that one can love an alcoholic. I think my father, were he alive, would have notified the world when his daughter braved the tyranny of advanced breast cancer.

After my telephone fight with my sister, my mother calls me. Word of our fight, I can see in retrospect, has flown over the wires. My brother-in-law has reported to her, my old friend and neighbor Ayrie tells me later. Mother does not mention this.

"How are you?"

I tell her about the white cell slump.

"How long will it last?"

"I don't know. There aren't that many women ahead of me who've had a peripheral stem cell rescue. They don't know." No one knows. I'm only about the eighth peripheral stem cell rescue they've done for breast cancer at that hospital.

My mother is quiet.

"We're not going for a cure, you know, Mom." I suddenly need her to know. "I'm going for *time*, treatment-free time."

"Oh, well," she says. "Cure. What's a cure? What if you go ten years without a recurrence? Would you call that a cure?"

I am speechless. I can't figure out what she is talking about. Why are we talking about ten years? Cancer reactivated in my spine within ten months.

We proceed with the usual talk, about my cousins, about the weather. But soon after we hang up, I call her back. "You know I've *already* had a recurrence, don't you?" I ask.

"No!"

I go patient. "In October 1992," I explain, "I had a biopsy of my vertebrae. The results were positive. I had an active tumor on L-2."

"Oh, that. I knew about that."

"Well, then, what *are* we talking about?" This is a phrase I say to myself often when my mother and I embark on one of these headlong conversations. This time, bless the blood cell slump, I say the words aloud. The barriers that usually shield me from the shame I feel about being angry, these lifelong barriers, have lowered. Cancer has changed me. I take more risks.

"If you knew about the recurrence, what *are* we talking about? Why are we speaking of going ten years, when I didn't even go ten months?"

"Well, how about now?"

"Now?"

"What do they tell you now?"

"I can't tell about now." (I'm in a slump right now. I told you that.)

She wants to know what my current bone scans show.

"I won't let them test me," I say, though this is not really true. The truth is that I have not let them test me *yet*. "The odds are too awful," I try to explain.

Jesus God, a can of worms. Pandora's box spilling like night crawlers from a Styrofoam cup. We are not meant to talk about odds. We are not meant to speak the unspeakable, that my odds are not good. The telephone wires are creepy with scary, slimy things that make us turn our backs and run from each other. She runs, I think, from the fact of my death. I run from my infantile conviction that my anger toward her will annihilate me.

"You're not thinking right."

My mother tells me that I am not thinking right. She says that. Aloud. Over the phone. To me, her daughter. I am not thinking right! She tells me that I should focus on the percentage of patients who make it three years. Thoughts like that will make me one of them.

These words *enrage* me. The mere assumption that good thoughts will affect the outcome of my life or death-revealing bone scans turns me ugly as Medusa. I have let my sister have it. Now it is my mother's turn.

"You are the only one who ever gets angry, Christina," my father told me once over the phone, when he had moved out to one of his motel home-away-from-homes, to drink, I suppose, and have women. "You are the only one who cares enough to get angry."

"What are we talking about—*thinking right?!*" I shout into the telephone. "Why didn't *thinking right* work in the beginning, when *none of us* thought that lump would turn out to be cancer?"

I am as enraged as any child whose mother misunderstands her. How *can* Mother suggest that I am not thinking right? How could my sister, busy as she is, strapped for money, overworked, swamped with troubles of her own, how could she not have found one minute to sign a Hallmark card, to make one telephone call, even a collect call, during all those weeks of isolation, during all those tedious months of recovery?

I need them, for the simple reason that they are my

mother and my sister. I need them to feel deep in their bones, the way Jonathan does, the pain I have endured and the grief I have felt. But instead, I go sarcastic. "OK, *you* have chemotherapy once a week for the rest of your life. Do that and tell me about thinking right!"

There is a great silence over the phone.

Finally I ask, "What's going on? I had a call from my sister who said that she didn't even know I'd been ill."

"No. She understood what I understood."

"And what was that?"

"That the bone marrow transplant would take care of your problem."

"Did you read that book I sent you?"

"Yes."

The book (*Bone Marrow Transplants: A Book of Basics for Patients and Their Families*) says: "The results of early clinical studies . . . [of] Stage IV breast cancer patients who had previously undergone intensive chemotherapy were encouraging. A remission was achieved in 27% of the patients. That remission, however, was of short duration."

Another paragraph describes cases *"with some remissions lasting three years or more"* (italics mine).

Three years. The books says maybe three years.

Finally I am silent. Rage has run its course. Extra innings will not bring an end to this standoff. We are not even in the same ball game. Maybe the only way they can care for me is to ignore my risk and tune out my suffering. I think that my mother thinks I have given up. I think she thinks if I were to go on having scans and tests, there would be more treatment choices available to me. She wants this to be true. It isn't.

My brother also calls. Reports of my temper have not reached him. We are talking about seeing each other when Jonathan and I, in our travel-while-we-can mode, visit Washington, D.C., where my brother lives. I tell my brother, who is the most realistic of them all, who has called infrequently but consistently throughout my ordeal, that our mother has told me that I did not have a recurrence.

"Maybe you'll have only *one* recurrence," he replies, kindly but ignorant. I sigh the deep sigh of the lonely. One recurrence is all it takes. I cannot breathe for the loneliness. I did not want to go this route without my family, my mother, my sister, my brother—my father is dead.

They are where I come from. They knew me first. They know things about me that no one else could know. They know without knowing how much they know. I want very, very much for my mother and sister and brother, *because* they are my mother and sister and brother, to understand exactly what my medical situation is, exactly what my prognosis is, exactly what my choices are. I need to think that the end of my life affects the continuation of their lives after I am gone. I am like a child again, the way I need them.

"But don't you see, Mom?" James says. "Your death won't change their lives the way it will change ours."

No, I had not seen that.

"Were you close before?" Judy, my sister-in-law, asks. I thought so. I guess not. No.

On Christmas Day 1992, the second Christmas in a row I orchestrated from the deep depletion of chemotherapy, Judy called. I'll never forget this. The remains of Christmas morning lay scattered throughout the living room. Every piece of furniture was decorated with scrunched-up wrapping paper. Jonathan and the children were doing their best at putting together the Christmas dinner that I have prepared for decades. Judy called and I, lying on top of our unmade bed, answered the phone.

I wish I could explain the density of a deep chemo-fog. On the one hand, I felt like me, a family member participating in our main holiday, temporarily reduced in energy. On the other, I felt every breath I took came through an asthmatic wheeze. I simultaneously understood and did not understand the effort Jonathan and the children were making, again, to sustain me in our cherished Christmas rituals.

We were in the bone marrow countdown then. My spine was well radiated. Cytoxan, adriamycin, and 5-Fluorouracil again coursed through my veins. Mom on the couch. Mom in bed. We even made 5-Fluorouracil one of our nasty charades words. Jonathan acted it out. Maggie got it. As soon as 1993 arrived, I would begin the daily blood pheresis to collect peripheral stem cells.

Judy knew this. Her attention had been constant and subtle: cards, a pair of earrings, a stained-glass treasure box from her new husband, Ed. I had a favor to ask. I needed to ask Judy, who is the caretaker for Jonathan's very elderly and very frail parents, about what would happen if one of them died while I was in the hospital. As I approached my own medically induced death and rebirth, I needed to know whether Jonathan could stay with me. Could she tolerate Jonathan at my side in the hospital, keeping my house and my children, rather than with her if Sam or Ruth died?

"Darling, of course!" she exclaimed. "You are his love. His place is at your side. If something happens here, of course we'll manage without him! You are not to worry about us!"

How like them I am, in spite of myself. No one, other than my mother and sister and brother and I, was underestimating my dire need. No one else underplayed my absolute risk. I had assumed that if Jonathan's father or mother died, he would go to them and I would manage on my own. That is how I was raised. That voice lives within me still.

Judy and I had an argument once, when I insisted that because her and Jonathan's mother is Jewish, they are Jewish. Judy, who joined the Episcopal church when she was a teen, was offended.

But this was Jewish warmth, coming to me over the phone on Christmas. It bears no resemblance to the cool Protestant pride in understatement that surrounded me

when I was growing up. I weep and weep for Judy's love. For her worry. Thank you, thank you, I sob. I'm sorry, I'm sorry.

"Oh, Christina, dear Christina," she says, again and again, not knowing what else to say. Nothing more is needed.

In nature there is the natural order and hierarchy of things. First there is birth, and then there is life, and last comes death. I turn the vegetable scraps into my compost heap. When drought comes to California for six years and I cannot water my garden, my plants die. Yesterday, by mistake, I stepped on the new tender shoots of a dahlia. An accidental death, unheralded. That, too, occurs.

God is a drunken phone call from my father in the night. Anger in Jonathan's gray face when the nurse insists on cleaning the infection around my Hickman catheter with alcohol. The doelike stillness in Leah's eyes when she knows I feel bad. James's rage. Ethan's gruffness. The ever-present tears in Maggie's eyes. Sophie's voice, so quiet over the phone that I think I have lost contact with her.

What I would give to see that presence, however fleetingly, in my mother, brother, and sister.

When they made their one visit to see me, during the very first course of my first chemotherapy, evidence of love and concern was all over my house. The children were attentive. The phone rang constantly. The refrigerator and freezer were full. But when my friend

David dropped by while I was out, they did not know to invite him in. When Nancy, soon to become Ethan's fiancée, came over, Mother did not think to notice her.

But she did count the cards I had on the mantelpiece and bookshelves and dining room table. "There were 157 of them!" she crowed to my old friend Linda, when they met again at Ethan's wedding. "Each with a personal note." Mother had counted them. She had walked through the downstairs of my house and counted the cards that came to me and noticed the letters written inside and never mentioned a word of this to me.

My sister cried during that phone call when I blew up at her. "I feel so guilty," she said. "The more I do nothing, the more immobilized I get."

I think besides guilt, there is envy. I can understand that. My sister, or anyone, well might feel envious of the attention I have had since this hideous diagnosis. Hideous as it is, cancer has bathed me in love. Healthy people, including me when I was one, can live life so unaware of love that we don't feel it until we trip over it. We don't see it until we fall flat on our faces. If my sister is envious, who can blame her? My mother has given me money during these cancer years, money to help with my bills while I could not work and to reduce the exorbitant burden of medical costs. Last year, both my sister and her husband were laid off. He works as a courier now, and she has taken a job at reduced salary. No one, including me, wrote them a get-well card when that happened. Mother has not sent them money.

But with God, you don't get perfect. You don't get easy. You just get all. And if you don't encompass all, you don't know God. You don't stand on the balcony when your husband is dying and yell "fuck you" toward heaven.

Amen.

13
FRUIT CITY BANANAS

Y OU'LL HAVE to watch out for me," I tell Maggie
and Jonathan at the dinner table, "because if I go
to visit my mother and she tells me *again* that I
haven't had a recurrence, I'll go Fruit City Bananas."

"You *are* such a dork, Mother. Fruit City Bananas.
Is that something you said in the sixties?"

"No, I just said it right now."

"Well, it's sixties."

"Seventies," Jonathan corrects.

Generations speak different languages. So do people
with cancer. We use the same words but we must have
different dictionaries. Things I say seem unintelligible
to people who live outside the cancer realm. Certain of
their phrases fall harshly on my ears.

If anyone second-guesses the decisions I've made
("If the odds are so bad, why go through a bone marrow
transplant?"), if anyone suggests that my realistic attitude
about my prognosis is wrong ("Hey, Christina, think pos-

itive"), or, worst of all, if anyone underplays the severity of the illness I have or of the treatment I have endured ("But I heard you got out of the hospital earlier than expected"), if any of this language is used, I go wild, nuts, FRUIT CITY BANANAS.

Here's a list:

1. The top of the list is everyone else's successful, early-detection, good-prognosis cancer story. I cannot see what Happy Rockefeller's bilateral mastectomy more than twenty-five years ago has to do with my metastatic disease. So what if my cousin had a lumpectomy and is doing fine?

"Not all news is bad," a friend tells me. "My mother had a biopsy recently and it was negative."

"How nice," I reply, wildness stirring inside.

"So maybe yours will be good."

"I've never had a negative biopsy," I say, turning away, the fruit beginning to spill out on the sidewalk where we are trying to talk.

One of my chums, a careful vendor at the Fruit City stand, leads me away. "He means well," she says. "He's worried about his mother." She puts her arm around me. "It's all so foreign to them. . . ."

"Arggh!" I say. How nice for "them," these speakers of my old language. I envy them. I'd trade places with them in a second. I'd really, really like to have had a negative biopsy, just once. I'd really like it if my next scans could show that I am cured.

2. The technicians in Radiation Oncology have a cheerful language. They use words like *beautiful, perfect, good*. Nice words to hear when I lie underneath that gigantic machine hoping against hope that the rays they will beam at me, soon, are hitting the exact and *beautiful* right spot, which underlies my *perfect* tattoos, which cover the surface of my *good* attitude.

They also never fail to tell me to "have a good weekend! See you Monday," even after meeting me a second time in eight months, this time to radiate my recently discovered spinal metastasis.

"And what are you doing for Thanksgiving?" one asks.

"Starting chemo again. Throwing up."

"Well, have a nice day."

3. We don't all speak the same language in my neighborhood, either. Five houses on this street have changed hands during the two-year course of my cancer treatments. All the new homeowners have spent months remodeling the houses they've bought, familiar houses that my family and I have been in and out of for years, borrowing tomato paste or vanilla, watering plants while the owners are away, tending their cats. Over the years we have kept each other's keys. We accept each other's UPS packages. During vacations we have collected the newspapers off each other's front steps.

Now, the new owners are updating the 1960s kitchens that my eye hadn't noticed were shabby. For the year before, during, and after my bone marrow transplant,

Dumpsters squatted at the curbside both uphill and down. Parking has been a bear. For months, the space in front of our house was crowded by some contractor's pickup. I've had to park elsewhere.

Most of the remodeling jobs are necessary upgrades. Even I am fluent enough to understand that. Kitchens built in the 1960s must be redone, termite damage repaired, leaky roofs fixed. But one neighborhood remodel is a downgrade. White shutters, usually left open, have been replaced with dark brown and kept closed. Perennial shrubbery has been replaced with short-lived annuals (a gardener making more money from owners who don't know the difference). A locked wrought-iron gate now blocks the front steps.

She is waiting for me when I pull my car into the space in front of her house. It is spring. I've been home from the hospital for a few months. I am still gray and bald and wearing my beefeater hat. My fingernails are in molt stage.

"You can't park here," she announces, her long red nails hard and perfect around the strap of her shoulder bag. She is thin and wears a slim leather coat. Her hair looks like TV.

I pull a puzzled face, though I think I am prepared for this fight; she left a note on my windshield yesterday. "What do you mean, I can't park here?"

"My husband can't get the big car into the garage." The big car is a red Jaguar, a V-12. She drives a modest gold Porsche.

"Why can't he?"

"You're too close."

Fruit City Bananas inside. I take a deep breath and attempt reasonable speech. "Look, I've left you plenty of room. I'm a foot and a half from your driveway."

"You're in the red zone."

"No it's not. It's a did-it-himself job. The guy who lived here before. Look, there's no police bud."

She looks at me as though I were speaking Swahili.

"I'm telling you, it's not a legal no-parking zone. The people who lived here before you just painted the curb red. See, there's no yellow SFPD logo. They also had the curb cut out to make the driveway look wider." All this is true. Parking precipitates turf wars, even in our can-I-borrow-an-egg neighborhood.

She doesn't speak Swahili. "Well, other people are living here now!"

"What difference does that make?" What the hell language is this?

"Why can't you park over there?" She points to an equally small space across the street between two other neighbors' driveways.

"Come on. We're neighbors." I was going to say that we might as well get used to each other. Then it occurred to me that she is likely to live here longer than I. The bananas pile up. "You can't just usurp the street. I've lived here twenty-five years," except I think I exaggerated and told her I'd lived here thirty. "I've parked in front of your house a million times and never got a ticket. I get a ticket for parking in my driveway and blocking the side-walk. I don't have a garage. You have a garage." But she remains within her own syntax. "Just go park somewhere else." Oh, the sense of entitlement! Why can't I feel that entitled? I am dead with envy. Maybe I am dying of envy. How simple to say things like that: "Go crowd another driveway. I just look out for myself." Advanced Narcis-sism 909. She makes it sound so easy.

"This is nuts!" I sputter, but already I am returning to the car to move it. "If I don't park in front of your house, someone else will. It's a public parking place!" I turn on the ignition and jerk the car through a U-turn to park across the street, in front of the old-time, familiar neighbors whose driveway is the narrowest and steepest on the block.

Then I carry my six bags of groceries twenty yards farther down the street, all the time thinking, "She can't speak to me like that. I've just had a bone marrow transplant!" I deserve a little help with the logistics of my grocery unloading. The world needs to make special considerations for me.

It doesn't.

4. Here's another Fruit City conversation, this one in-tending the kindest of thoughts.

"Your husband must be a very nice man. He must have a wonderful reputation."

Gerda at my bank says this. She has just finished helping me switch $40,000 from the Christina Middlebrook Bone Marrow Fund to a checking account. It is time to pay the bills.

Money for the fund has come pouring in, from friends, neighbors, parents of the children's friends, old high school and college buddies, distant relatives. Martha and Lynn, who orchestrated the appeal, would come to the hospital and read me amusing and serious letters from friends and relatives I had not seen in decades. They remembered me. They liked me enough, still, to send money because I needed it. Some of Lynn's friends and family who had hardly met me gave to the fund because Lynn was so upset. This is one of the nicest things that has ever happened to me.

But few of them know Jonathan. We haven't been married that long. I've known Lynn since she worked for my children's father, Martha since her daughter started kindergarten with Maggie.

"The money came in so quickly," Gerda comments. "I've never seen so much money collected in such a short time."

Gerda was quite helpful to Jonathan and Martha in setting up the fund, I remember. But she doesn't get that *I'm* the patient. *I'm* Christina Middlebrook. She doesn't get that people sent money because they liked me. I mean, if Gerda got sick, and her friends and neighbors and the kind people at the bank where she worked contributed to a fund, would that be because they admired Gerda's husband? Can't women be associated with money? Does it all have to come by means of men? Poor Gerda. Some of the most sexist comments I have heard come, unwittingly, from women.

"Your husband must be a very nice man. He must have a wonderful reputation." I have been invisible throughout the whole interaction. She has no concept of me as a living, functioning, competent person.

Silenced again, speechless, I smell fruit. Bananas? Apples? Fruit City close by.

When I go home and repeat this story to Jonathan, he just puts his arms around me. He *is* a very nice man.

5. Consider Margaret Deansley, M.D., a most articulate luncheon speaker at a Northern California Cancer Institute conference on "A Neglected Issue: The Sexual Side Effects of Breast Cancer Treatment, Part II." Dr. Deansley, the program reads, "is well known for her presentations on early detection and patient-physician communication. She lectures throughout the country and is appreciated for her candor, humor, and practicality."

Evidently many people think Dr. Deansley is just a stitch. She gets lots of laughs. She has a way with words and says things like "I'm a doctor—I can say the word *penis*" and "Admit it. We've learned that when it comes to sex, slippery is good." She refers to having had her breast "thrown in the trash in 1968." Her solution to the breast cancer crisis has a lot to do with lingerie. One of the things she advises, to improve our sex lives, is to go to the baby department at Saks and buy a pretty little lace baby pillow. Then, during intercourse, she suggests, we could slip this pretty little pillow, our "treat to ourselves," between our lover's chest and our empty mastectomy site.

I don't know what language we're hearing. A *baby* pillow? The solution is a *baby pillow?!*

"For heaven's sake," she exclaims, "80 percent of us with this disease are going to do just fine." I look around the crowded lunch room and estimate there are about 300 women here. Certainly some are health care professionals, but the vast majority are here because they have breast cancer. From Deansley's statistics I calculate that maybe 160 of the 200 breast cancer women here "will do just fine." So that leaves 40, *40* of us who won't. And Dr. Deansley is making boob jokes. People are laughing.

"How many of you," this charismatic speaker asks, "are dependent on the use of a prosthesis?"

A few dozen of us, including me, raise our hands.

"Well, that's not very many, is it?" she cheerleads.

At the table where I sit, my dear friend Faith, who has an inflammatory cancer, says, "Why is it that after I attend one of these conferences I feel more lonely?"

The goddamned bananas are rotting. *Forty of us are not doing well. Forty of us* in this very room! Are we meant to quietly excuse ourselves, to leave the party so that the others can remain happy by not knowing about us? Faith feels lonely. I am dumb, mute, lost in a city of fruit.

6. I guess that if you haven't been there, you just can't learn it. You can't get it from a book, or from interviews. You can only speak the language by living there, even if you are a reporter trying to make a story. Here's an example from an article in the *San Francisco Chronicle,* August 28, 1993, about a reunion of bone marrow transplant survivors: "After beginning her treatment (a bone marrow transplant) Wetzel continued to live as normal a life as possible, even going home at one point to throw a party for 50 people." Could someone translate that for me, please?

Let's see. I, in the midst of the bone marrow transplant, pack up my IV pole, the six bags of platelets, whole blood, and medicines, stumble out of my isolated, reverse air-circulation room, and *go home to mingle with fifty happy guests.* My system is so loaded with Dilaudid that I make no sense at all. Nevertheless, a wonderful time is had by all ... except the patient. Someone sneezed. She succumbed. Had a positive attitude, though. Never once let that outcast, cancer, interfere with the living of a "normal" life.

Then, miraculously, communications do occur. I speak. Someone understands. My new next-door neighbors obligingly prune and shape their loquat tree so that the low winter sun can reach my daffodils. I don't have to explain that I can't climb ladders and wield loppers. New neighbors on the other side take photos of my garden from their kitchen and give me copies when I am still quarantined within the house.

Neither knew me before I had cancer. They speak the lingo, anyway.

I remember the day when one of them learned what was going on with me. We were getting out of our parked cars at the same time, and Mary remarked that I looked very tired. This would have been when I was just reentering radiation therapy, only a month after Mary and her family had moved in. She and her eight-year-old daughter, Katie, listened while I explained why I looked so bad.

"I'm a cancer patient," I told them. "I've just started up a new course of radiation."

"I see," Mary said. "That must be rough."

I spoke to Katie then, who was standing behind her mother on the sidewalk in front of our two houses. I knew how often we would be looking at each other over our backyard fence.

"I'm going to have to take some medicine that makes my hair fall out," I said. Katie nodded solemnly.

I never felt the foreign language problem with her after that simple conversation, initiated by Mary's sensitive observation that saved me the embarrassment of wondering what my new neighbors would think when they saw me and my bald head gardening in the backyard.

The spring was warm. I was outdoors often in my frail, posttransplant state. On each side of the fence they asked, matter-of-factly, how I was that day. I found it easy to speak the simple truth. "My counts have been too low for me to go out, but I am better now," or, "Today's just a terrific day." Being able to speak straightforwardly to them has been a blessing. These people did not even know me before my diagnosis.

I never dreamed the difficulty people have finding a way to speak about cancer, serious illness, death. Sometimes others' need to minimize what has happened startles me. An old friend, a good friend, commented offhandedly that he would not attend a talk I gave at work about how I delegated my analytic practice when I took ill because, he said, "it's too depressing."

Others comment to me, when I respond to the "How are you?" with a serious answer, that they too get tired, that they also have difficulty remembering, that they also must watch their diets. If I say my feet hurt (another unmentioned side effect), they tell me about someone else's arthritis.

I am astonished. Did I used to speak that way myself? Probably. I remember telling a friend, before, that breast cancer is a "good cancer."

In a dream I am tossed into a rough bay. I am in peril. I must swim against the current to reach the shore. I worry that the young man who is with me, who cannot swim, will pull me under. People on the shore can see us. They are very concerned, very worried. They cannot help. After arduous effort I reach the shore with the young man in tow. We crawl up the beach to a terrace. People are sitting under umbrellas, drinking and eating. They have watched our perilous swim. Though it is evident that they want to help us, they speak only Arabic.

I know words in a dozen languages, but not a single one of Arabic.

This week Ricki, from my bone marrow transplant group, had a bad blood test. We share the same doctor. I find her leaning against the wall outside his office.

"What is it?" I ask.

"My CA15-3 is up."

"Oh, no." A CA15-3 is an antigen marker. Anything under 30 is safe. Mine has been around 11. "Is it high?"

"Yeah," a sigh.

"*High* high?"

"Yeah."

"Tell me."

"172."

"Oh, Ricki, I'm sorry. That goddamned test."

We are silent. Ricki looks stricken. I feel stricken. Not Fruit City Bananas–stricken. Just clear-eyed, bad-news–stricken.

"Would a hug help?" I ask, not knowing Ricki all that well.

"I think so."

I hug her and tell her that I love her. "We're all in this together," I say.

Two cancer patients, two bone marrow transplant survivors, talking. This is the only language I can speak.

Later, I am present when Ricki informs others of her bad news.

"Oh, that was someone else's test. They got it mixed up."

"You know those tests don't mean anything. Probably the vitamins you're taking."

"You'll be fine."

Jesus God! Here we go again. The whole goddamned vegetable stand!

Here is the enraging irony. When I do die, when this fucker disease does come back, I will reap no benefit from my "I-told-you-so" revenge. I will be dead. And some probably will buzz at my memorial that I made my disease come back by admitting that it would.

What I want is this. I want the well-entrenched American denial system to change. We are taught that when a person informs us "I am dying" or "I'm in deep shit here," we are to respond by saying, "Oh, no. No, you're not. You'll be fine."

I want a different response. I want interest and curiosity. I want the same concern I'd get if I said that I had been laid off from a job or had broken a leg. I want someone to say "God, how awful. How're you doing?" I want someone to ask, "What's it like?"

Scrumptious. Delicious. Ambrosia for the gods.

14

TESTS

———————— ❦ ————————

B AD GUYS in Iran, the ones who take hostages, I read, take an innocent American, a librarian or some such whom they have held captive for three years, they take him out of his cell into a courtyard and tell him that the moment of his death has arrived. The firing squad assembles, the rifles are loaded, shouldered, all for him to see. Then he is backed against the wall and blindfolded. Loud noises in another language, commands probably, the unmistakable cock of rifles, assault his fine-tuned ears. Every sense alert, every breath his last, he waits. When the hostage's knees buckle, his tormentors laugh and drag him back to his cell.

Periodically an execution actually takes place, I read. A hostage is shot. This keeps the experience real. This is the torture.

Every six months I go through the same thing. I

depart my cell on an empty stomach at 7:00 A.M., due at the hospital at 8:00. They line me up beneath the big CT scanner that reports the news of my life or death, warn me not to move, insist that I keep my arms crooked above my head. I wait. One and a half hours I wait. Inside the control room, absorbed in their technology, they forget that I am a human being. My arms grow numb. My shoulders are locked in pain.

The tech laughs when he is finished. "A long time, huh? We kind of lose track of time."

Then, after I am dressed, I ask for the verdict. Is this an execution or not? May I look at the film? The radiologist shows me my sacroiliac.

"No, not that," I tell him. "Find L-2. That's where the metastasis is."

He rifles through the clumsy sheets. "Metastasis?" he asks. "Oh, here. Yes. There's metastasis."

I fish my reading glasses out of my purse and scrutinize the gray and yellow shapes. I am not seeing what I want to see. The vertebra before me does not resemble the bright, whole vertebra I have been visualizing. L-2 has changed since last February, when my oncologist told me my scans were as good as he could hope for.

"The cortex," I tell the radiologist. "It looks pretty good, doesn't it?"

"Yes."

"But maybe it's getting a little fuzzy over here?" Really, I don't know what the hell I am talking about.

I'm just babbling. Who knows what thoughts pass through the mind of an innocent librarian as he waits against a foreign wall? All I know is that I don't like what I am seeing. Too much gray, too many shadows, a bigger shadowy area than I remember from February. The shadows overlap like puddles on glass. This is one fucked-up vertebra I am seeing. "What do you think?" I ask the radiologist who has now gone inscrutable.

"I'd have to make a comparison with a former scan." His voice has changed to a monotone.

I laugh, charmingly, I think. "Sure, of course. You aren't as familiar with these vertebrae as I am." Ha-ha-ha. I'll let you take a little while to catch up. Sure. Get back to me later. I smile. "Thanks."

"Are you under treatment for this?"

"You bet."

I leave. Jonathan is waiting by the stack of used little pillowcase things they call gowns. I'm wearing one, of course, as part of the humiliation. "Bad," I tell him. "Those were bad, awful pictures." His face sags. "Everything's changed. I didn't like them. I'm upset."

Then we go upstairs for round two, Nuclear Medicine, where I'll have a MUGA, to test my heart. My heart still feels the effects of my confinement, from the adriamycin and mitoxantrone that poisoned me in order to save my life. More paperwork. Do I have my pass? Plastic smiles. The secretary can't spell Middlebrook. Finally, when I'm actually on the inside, where more big machines line the walls, I tell the tech she is going to have to access my port because I don't have any veins. She gives me an airline stewardess smile.

"She didn't understand a word I said," I tell Jonathan, who has noticed. My sneer gets the attention of all three techs. They come to attention. I have risked offending them. For a moment, I don't care.

"What is it?" they ask. I repeat. The techs dither and discuss. They don't know how to inject medicine through the Porta-Cath I've had embedded in my left clavicle since my veins gave out in 1992.

"We'll just try a vein first," they tell me with smiles I'd like to punch, but I must be careful. Standing here, with the best of nuclear medicine aimed straight at my heart, I am dependent on their good humor. I must not provoke them.

"Oh, no," I am begging now, "we'll just go through what I always go through. You'll poke me for half an hour, and then you'll tell me you can't get a vein." My voice is on the sing-song edge of a whine.

"Then you had better go down to the Cancer Center. We don't have the right equipment." They stand there, stupid, resolute, following orders.

"*He'll* do it," I say, pointing to my husband, the English professor, who has lifted a packet of Porta-Cath paraphernalia from the lab in the Cancer Center.

Their *macha* bluster crumbles immediately. Face is saved. We are all friends again. "*He* knows how? Great."

Jonathan lays me out on a stretcher and pretends he has accessed my port ten thousand times. The first two attempts, with me prone, fail. Then he remembers to sit me up. On the third, as I am upright, I feel the needle slip into place. We smile to the tech who has been handing him syringes. "There, see. Easy." Jonathan's hands are sweaty, but we keep that fact a little secret between ourselves.

"They give you a course in how to do that?" the tech asks.

"Yeah." What liars we have become.

After the MUGA, I return to Radiology for a chest X ray and listen to the secretary there tell me about the time she had an MRI, which is really worse than a CT scan. She tells me I didn't need to fast before I came in.

When we get home, I am shaky with dread. The Cancer Center maintains a peacekeeping force, a neutral zone where I can contact an angel, one of the two advice nurses. I have seen the ominous CT scan, a pall that turns every day into an execution day. But I figure that if I can get a call through to the advice nurse, there is one last hope. Through her I can get my latest antigen count. If my antigens are holding, there is still hope.

The blessed advice nurse calls back within an hour simply to tell me that my blood results are not yet available. Imagine that! I am still a human being. Tomorrow morning, she tells me. I'll hear from her tomorrow morning. The next morning I hear nothing. Jonathan and I take the silence as a sign that hostilities have increased. A white flag can travel only so far into a war zone. The advice nurses cannot save *all* the threatened foreigners. By Friday afternoon, at least two of my friends know that I have relapsed. I haven't called anyone, but those who call me hear the great sadness in my voice. We are all crying.

"I think I'm going to say a prayer," offers one. "I don't pray much but. . . "

"So what can you pray for?" I ask, short-tempered.

"I can pray for the CT to come out right."

"It doesn't work that way. You can't pray for something not to be what it is."

"I can pray for whatever I want to pray for."

"Why don't you pray that I can take what comes with grace? Pray for that."

Linda, my old friend, says, "I'll keep my toes and fingers crossed, seeing as I don't believe in sending messages anywhere else."

We are all trying, all doing our best to change this horror into something unhorrible.

The hostage situation continues. Late in the day word gets through from the riots in the streets. The advice nurse tells me there has been a bureaucratic delay, a deadlock among the diplomats. She tells me that my antigen count has tripled and that my MUGA is way below normal.

"Yeah, I figured that," I tell her. "I saw my CTs. My antigen count was way down three months ago."

"I see." She is quiet. "I'm sorry to have to bring you bad news."

"Listen, you guys are great. You always get back to me when I call. Really. I've got no problem with you." I mean it. Can you imagine a nurse calling just to tell me that my lab tests *aren't ready yet?* I'm happy to see the Red Cross anytime. We adore the UN peacekeepers.

Two things are for sure. My body is trying harder to fight off cancer (tripled antigens), and my heart isn't ejecting blood into my system very efficiently (MUGA below normal). I don't give a damn about my heart. The oncologist said he could take care of that, easy. I'm not sure a cardiologist would say the same, but we are into oncology here, and heart problems don't count.

I call back my praying friend. "Oh, shit!" she says. "I thought I could manage the CT, but I don't think I can pray down the antigens too."

Awful weekend. The M16s, loaded and in the hands of maniacs, are pointing straight at me. I feel a great pressure of time. I want to finish my writing, and finish refinishing the furniture, and weed the garden to perfection. We decide not to go anywhere over Labor Day weekend. I don't want to attend the September reunion of bone marrow transplant survivors, and I don't think I'll go to my thirty-fifth high school reunion, either. I just want to lie forever in the arms of my sweet husband, except the universe has conspired to send undiagnosable pain into his right shoulder—a degenerative disk? bursitis? autoimmune disease?—and he can't control his weakened right arm—a stroke? But we ignore all those calamitous possibilities because my CT scan was so awful, and because he won't die from a pain in his shoulder.

I won't have time to buy a new wristband for my watch, and there is no sense in ordering any of the clothes I saw in the fall catalogs. I'm going to lose my hair again, just when I have finally retrieved the hair I used to have, a bitter loss because even *I* have been thinking, of late, that I look good again. I look good for nought. What's the point? No matter what treatment I undertake, it is going to make me ugly again, and gray, and bloated. And it is not going to work for very long.

"We offer this not as a cure," the doctor has explained, many times, "but as a palliative. To delay the inevitable."

"I know," I tell him. I have a number of friends in the palliative/inevitable stage.

I have to get my book written before they start me up on adriamycin again, because I can't think on adriamycin. But they won't do that, will they, because adriamycin is what has messed up my heart? Taxol, that cruel menace, maybe it will be taxol. Throwing up. No hair. Side effects.

I give Jonathan the envelope in which I've stuffed dozens of articles about nonchemotherapy treatments for metastatic cancer. Deborah died within weeks of her relapse. Ricki is on taxol now, weak, no hair. I list my friends with bone metastases, make a mental note to call them, but not until after Thursday—after all, I am not a radiologist, so I should wait to hear what my doctor has to say before I consult with them about all the treatment options they've explored.

Another friend calls, and I am so upset that Jonathan takes the phone to tell her that we are entering a new phase. Then she is so upset that she calls another friend who calls me in tears.

"This is my karma," I tell one of them. "I've got to figure out how to go with my karma."

James has returned from his year in London. On Sunday he comes by and hangs around the garden eating the peas off the vine. They are perfect right now, as sweet as life. I follow him from stem to stem, driving him crazy telling him which peas are fat enough to pick and happy as can be that he is eating green vegetables willingly. He notes my perpetual limp, asks how my knees are. I remind him that it is my feet that hurt all the time, and they are fine, fine, fine. I am not going to tell him *anything,* not even that I have had these tests, until I know for sure, on Thursday, and then, God save me, how am I going to tell him, again? Through my terror I hear him chat about his work, his sister, his upcoming visit with his father. He is twenty-four, a man, gorgeous lolling over the armchair in my living room. One word from me can destroy all this. One word.

Maggie calls on Sunday too. Maggie, now nineteen and definitely on her own, went *skydiving,* Lord have mercy, on Friday. I have combed the *San Francisco Chron-*

icle for news of a wayward skydiving event up in the San Juan Islands. Found nothing.

"Hey!" I shout into the phone. "You're still alive!"

"What are you talking about, Mom?"

"You. You didn't crash! How was it?"

"Oh, the jump. It was great. Listen, Mom. I can't talk long. But I lost my wallet. You have to send me my spare driver's license."

The reason Maggie has a spare driver's license is that she lost her wallet before and then found it. She still needs a mother, I think. She can jump out of planes, and work for a living, and manage a house now with her friends, but she still needs a mother to send her her spare driver's license. I can't stand the news I am going to have to tell them. I can't stand being jerked out of their lives, again and forever. I sob when my daughter is safely off the phone. When should I tell them? Next week all three will be together with their father. Would that be a good time? I could call their father first, before they arrive. I could tell them as I drive them to the airport. They could commiserate on the plane. Then their father could meet their plane with wide parental arms, the only arms they'll have. Yes, that's what I'll do.

Somebody call Amnesty International!

Monday I get a letter from Ethan with a copy of the essay he is writing to apply for a residency in pediatrics. He wants me to edit it for him. He also wants me to dig up the essay he wrote to get into medical school.

He too needs me, still. He is twenty-six years old and married and in the fourth year of medical school. Yet I am the only person on Earth who knows where his medical school essay is! Better change that. Better go through all these drawers and boxes. I should send their father all their stuff, labeled, dated, but he'd lose it. I could include my final letter in each carton. No. I must let them go. I must trust the years I have invested in them. They *will* manage. They *will* help one another. Jonathan will be here.

Jonathan tells me that he is going to bury my ashes in the garden under a plaque with all five of my names on it, as I once requested. Frederika Christina Ross Cutts Middlebrook. Frederika is my mother. Ross, my father. Cutts is my children's name. Middlebrook is my husband. I am Christina, only Christina. Maybe I should change my request to that one, single name. Me.

The plaque is going to say "She becomes the garden that she loved." He tells me that at dusk, while we sit together in our scruffy jeans, tired and dirty from the weekend's work, on the deck Jonathan has built outside our kitchen. He has been pouring concrete for a retaining wall. His hair has grown too long at the fringes, bits of dead leaves are sticking to the top of his sweaty, bald head. Jonathan is so goddamned redneck and poetic and sexy and beautiful. He is drinking bourbon and listening to country music. He has glued an American flag onto the dashboard of his Ford, next to a frog, next to a holder for his shades, next to a pad of paper where he writes down thoughts and chores when he waits at a red light. Second to me, he loves words best. I am in awe of that word, *becomes*. It says everything I want said about me and what I believe in, about my presence and my compost. His eyes are filled with tears all the time now, and we cling together, except that his shoulder hurts so much we can't cuddle in bed. I grieve for how little time I have left to feel his skin next to mine all night long.

Monday night equals Breast Cancer Support Group night. This night we are meeting here, at my house. My group understands, immediately, what it is to be dragged out into that courtyard on so-called execution day. They've been there themselves, endured the lineup, the wait, the humiliation that leaks from every pore. Each of the women in my support group has lived the days that I am living now. Each has waited for the end or for the release, not knowing which to prefer. They do not doubt me when I tell them what the CTs showed.

"I wish I could just say don't worry," Faith cries. "I wish I could say it will be all right. I know I can't." No one rushes in to reassure me. We know that, routinely, a hostage is killed. Some of our friends. Some of our group members.

I apologize for making them cry and they get mad at me, kind of, for my apology. I can't stand that my news hurts other people, but the group tells me that is what love is, and I know it.

When they leave I check the messages on my answering machine. The last is from the angel of mercy herself—Chris, the advice nurse. She is calling to let me know, now, so I won't have to wait the three centuries until Thursday, that my chest X ray is fine and that my CT scan is unchanged from February. Yes, my MUGA is low and my antigens elevated, but from the point of view of the radiologist who compared my CT scans, everything looks good.

What? Jonathan is lying on the bed, reading. He puts his book down. "Play that again," he says. I do. We heard it right the first time. Everything looks good.

"I am such an asshole," I tell him. "My God what I have put you through these five days." He is smiling. "I am so sorry!"

He sits up and stretches. "It's okay," he grins.

"No, I mean it. I've been horrible."

"Hey," he says, so gently. "I get to keep you for a while."

"God. Dear, good God. I have a few phone calls to make."

I have four friends to call, as well as all the members of my group. I can't believe what I have done to them. "I am a fine Jungian Analyst," I tell them, "and a fine writer. But I have been a crazy friend and a shitty radiologist!"

"It's torture," they tell me. "People go nuts when they are being tortured."

Six months from now, I'm going to go through it all again.

15
COOKED CARROTS

F AITH WONDERS why she doesn't feel enlightened
the way all the other cancer survivors who tell their
stories do. Other cancer survivors, the ones who
write books, who speak of cancer having rearranged
their priorities, bettered their relationships, made them
grateful for each day. She asks whether anyone else in
our breast cancer support group feels thus enlightened.

Enlightenment. I try to picture white clouds on a
blue sky—what Jonathan calls a Jesus sky. Italian post-
Renaissance paintings are filled with Jesus skies. Enlightenment, I think, equals peace, serenity, tranquillity. The
list is long: gratitude, awe, acceptance. I hate that list.

So I tell the group. "Well, I don't eat cooked carrots
anymore."

It's true. I don't. My mother and grandmother
taught me to eat them and I have, for fifty-three years.
I'm not going to, ever again. Soups, stews, pot roast—
in this house all will be cooked without carrots.

"Sometimes I think smart people are very stupid," my friend Don tells me when I report this realization to him. We are eating at a restaurant and I have made an elaborate show of shoving aside the carrots. "You're a smart person," he says, "and you had to have Stage IV cancer and a bone marrow transplant before you even *knew* you didn't like cooked carrots."

And before I even knew which people I didn't like. And which things I didn't really want to do—like work full-time or spend money eating in restaurants three times a week because I am too exhausted to cook; I don't like not having time to go to the grocery store. And before I could overcome the disapproval of my favorite, mainstream doctor to apply for a maverick T antigen study, before I could take up acupuncture and Chinese medicine.

I had to have Stage IV cancer and a bone marrow transplant before I could realize how frightened I am of my *own* anger, how deep a critic fuels the voice within my *own* head. And before I could really *know,* down to the soles of my shoes, that nothing I will ever do can make people become better or worse people, more or less lovable. The surrender that accompanies these revelations is wonderfully relieving. With surrender has come, for the first time, the understanding that I too, for better or worse, am loved.

If this new self-knowledge is an indication of enlightenment, then enlightenment is not all it's cracked up to be. Jonathan's shoulder pain turns out to be bra-

chioplexitis, a debilitating virus. For months he has suffered pain, lack of coordination, tingling in his hands,
and weakness in his shoulders. He tells me, mournfully,
that he is afraid of aging.

"Big deal!" I say. Anger is red-hot in my voice.

We are lying in bed. He turns away from me and
pulls the covers up over his ears.

"You're just feeling sorry for yourself," I tell him,
almost spitting.

"Can't you find any empathy?" he asks. "Just one
shred?"

"Sure, when there is something to feel empathic
about."

Ugh.

When, finally, a doctor diagnosed him, we learned
that it may take two years, if ever, for his nerves to
regenerate. This is not a good prognosis. A good wife,
the unenlightened wife I once was, might worry or at
least feel solicitous. Not me. I think, two years! Terrific!
Wouldn't it be fabulous if I could be reconstituted in
two years?!

Then, cold cruelty changes to panic. I am really terrified that, in pain and weak as he is, my devoted and
reliable husband will not be able to take care of me
anymore. I have counted on him remaining strong, and
young.

Approaching enlightenment, but only after a few
days have passed, I can admit this dearth of empathy,
first to myself and then to him. I can say the words

aloud: "I am just too envious that you still consider aging!"

Jonathan nods. "I can understand that," he allows.

How thankless for him to live with someone who can *always* win the who-is-suffering-the-most competition.

Enlightenment.

What else? I wonder. What other possible revelations have come my way? Often I ask myself how I want to live what remains of my life. I ask myself, "Am I ready to die tomorrow?" When I can't sleep, which is frequently, I ask myself that question. "What if this is the last sleep of my life?" Before cancer, to induce sleep, I would list all fifty states in alphabetical order. When that became as easy as reciting a nursery rhyme, I listed all the state capitals in alphabetical order. I used to fantasize a quiz show that would drop that question on its contestants. I, prepared to win millions, would begin: Alabama, Alaska, Arizona, Arkansas. And for *advanced* contestants: Albany, Annapolis, Augusta (Georgia), Augusta (Maine). The audience, the *world,* would be stunned by my organizational brain.

Now, at 3:00 A.M., when I ask myself whether I am ready to die, I list the things undone, in alphabetical order (no, that last is a joke). But if there is something undone, and I find myself alive in the morning, I will do it. I will say aloud to Susan or Lynn or Chauncy or Ruth or Valerie or Martha or John or Don (the list is endless—longer even than the list of enlightenments)—to each and every one of my friends I will say what may have remained unsaid. I love you. I admire you. Without you, I could not have survived thus far. I do not want my children to have to wait until they are seriously ill to hear from me that I love them. I do. I tell them so.

I write letters (including nearly three hundred thank-you notes, for dinners, flowers, letters, books, contributions to my bone marrow fund) to friends I have not seen for decades and may never see again, to authors whose books I admire, and also to thoughtless hospital administrators, like the ones who forgot to tell us when the Comprehensive Cancer Center moved to the other side of town.

Other things undone: a perfect will, a list of assets in the family trust, continual update of my life insurance, this book, the book that Jonathan and I wrote when we traveled through Eastern Europe the summer after communism collapsed. Finished but never published, the book I wrote when I divorced my children's father. Finished but needing rewrite, the memoir I wrote after we buried Grama, Daddy's mother, and Mother bribed the mortician to slip the urn containing Daddy's ashes into the foot of Grama's coffin.

Also undone: a Christmas present for my sister. Generosity rose from me last December like an underground spring, as welcome as an oasis in the desert. I did not think I would feel generosity again. Of course I sent my sister a Christmas present. Of course I wrote her again. Is this enlightenment? Forgiveness? If enlightenment allows me to be a cruel and envious wife, perhaps my sister can be a disinterested and inattentive sister. Does enlightenment evolve from my recovery, from the fact that now, nearly two years post-transplant, I am physically stronger? My reserves are deeper. Forgiveness no longer feels impossible. I can forgive her. I can even forgive *myself* for having been so mad.

After an adulthood of paying mortgages and tuitions, I have begun to spend money on myself. I take my credit card out of storage and head for the mall. I work the mall from one end to the other until, when I am trying to purchase a silk blazer, the computers react. Nordstrom's will not accept my card. Too much activity, the computer says. Too much activity after too much quiet. The saleswoman demands picture identification. I give her my driver's license, but the photo taken last year does not resemble me.

"It's me," I insist. "Me. My card." (I'm using it again, I want to tell her. You can't imagine why. You can't imagine where I've been.) "That *is* me in the picture." (Me with the buzz cut, the radical femme ID). "I *know* it doesn't look like me, but it is."

The clerk and I stare at each other. I fantasize the uproar I will make if Nordstrom's refuses my card. "Discrimination against cancer patients!" the headline will scream. As the clerk taps more entries into the register, I fantasize ripping off my blouse and bra to *show* her. How dare Nordstrom or my bank deny me credit!

The same fantasy enthralls me when, shaky with exhaustion, I choose to use the shower stall for the disabled at my swim club. I am certain that some self-righteous goody-goody will challenge my disability, my right to use this stall with its bench for sitting and its convenient, hand-held shower nozzle. "Fuck you!" I'll yell at her skepticism. "I have Stage IV cancer and I've been through hell!"

I would not have said these things, before. I might have thought them but never dared say them. Could I say them now? I think so. I think they would spill out of my mouth. Is this enlightenment or bitchiness? Self-assertion or flat-out meanness? Perhaps enlightenment lies in not waiting to know the difference. Perhaps there is no difference. I can forgive myself if I am wrong. If I can forgive myself, perhaps I can forgive all the jerks who said wrong things when I was sick. Oh, God, maybe they weren't jerks.

But there is no standoff with the salesclerk. No challenge at the swimming pool. Just me, my *un*enlightened self, still incredulous that I have been as ill as I have, therefore still slow to differentiate the voices inside my head from the ones outside. If *I* cannot believe how sick I am, how can anyone else? I long for a stranger to fight with. An oblivious, insensitive jock with a mitt large enough to field my fury.

The saleswoman at Nordstrom says she can recognize me in the driver's license photo. She can match the post-chemo face to the one that looks at her over the cash register. Perhaps something in my eyes or manner reveals to her that I am still the same person. Don told me that once, when I was reeling with bad news. "Christina," he said. "You are still the same person you've always been." I lose track of that fact. It takes a friend to remind me. Bless my friends, bless them all.

In addition to becoming combative and acquisitive, I am becoming conniving. Even in the very beginning, during my first go-round with chemotherapy, I connived. I signed up for an insurance policy—one of those sleazy ones that comes by telephone solicitation. The premiums are high, $42 a month for $13,250 worth of life insurance on a policy that promises to "take care of my bills" should I die. When the unfortunate salesman called, I said, "Ha! You would never insure *me!*" They did. Fools. I figure it will take 26.2896 years at $42 a month for me to lose money on that policy.

So now I am *obliged* to have a $13,000 balance on my credit card before I am too sick to go on spending. Clothes, shoes, cashmere sweaters, a new stereo system, a new TV. Season tickets to the theater. I *have* to spend money. So far, I'm only up to $6,000. Entrenched habits from precancer days force me to make a payment every month, but the balance climbs and my budding enlightenment lets it.

A woman with advanced breast cancer, given three to six months, rents a condominium overlooking San Francisco Bay for $3,600 a month. A beautiful place, I am told, right on the water, with commanding views. But she keeps on living . . . and living and living.

Hearing that story I laugh a diabolical laugh, a fall-on-the-floor, weeping, wet-your-pants laugh.

I can see Mephistopheles dancing around her wall-to-wall carpeting. He skates across her Corian countertops and leaps across her empty living room (she didn't buy furniture) to block the fabulous view of San Francisco with which he seduced her.

I too have made deals with the devil. He tells me I am living on borrowed time. So, I borrow. I want the bedroom ceiling, which is shedding paint like a gruesome skin disease, fixed and painted. I want the threadbare carpet on the stairs replaced. I want new casement windows and a roof that doesn't leak. I want voice mail, a printer for my computer. I want the couch reupholstered. I want all these things *now*. The virtue of waiting has evaporated.

Jonathan and I have used the traveling miles I accrued from my wild spending—Have my shopping sprees and new familiarity with shopping malls put me in the American mainstream at last?—to visit people I have not visited in decades and to see new places. Is this the devil inside, materialistic and fat with greed? Or is it the voice of enlightenment reminding me that *all* time is borrowed time?

A couple of months after the bone marrow transplant, Jonathan and I spent a weekend in Death Valley. I wanted to see the desert in bloom. At first all I saw were the rocks and sand of a barren wasteland. My hurried glance was blind. Then, as patience descended, I found the tiny colors that bloom under rocks and in sandy crevices. Desert flowers bloom in *inches,* half and quarter inches. Life is that small in Death Valley. Where the water is, where the tourist buses stop, the scene comes in square miles. Japanese tourists in tuxedos, gowns, and parasols—this is true!—tiptoe out onto the salt flats, then tiptoe back to their air-conditioned buses. Bloom and fade, the life and death of the desert, go unheralded except by those who have learned to see.

A tiny gain in enlightenment for me here, discovering how to see a desert in bloom. Enlightenment is turning out to be no bigger than a petal.

Six months post-transplant, Jonathan went on sabbatical. My hair had reappeared for the second time, short and curly, revealing lots of forehead, time repeating time. We took a car trip from Chicago to Washington, D.C. My mother had not come to see me; I went to her, knowing I'd never visit her in her house again. I wanted to say that, aloud, but we never spoke of my illness while I was there, nor of my bone marrow transplant. I could not break the silence. Enlightenment failed. We spoke of . . . nothing.

From Chicago, we made an eleven-hour, nonstop drive to Brockport, New York, cold and north and miles from anywhere, so that I could see where my college roommate Judith has lived for the thirty years since we last lived together. Judith, I think, is disinterested in the very concept of enlightenment. She has an adamant matter-of-factness that I quite admire. We know exactly why I am driving so far out of my way to see her. If I don't visit her home now, I will never see it.

In Stockbridge, Massachusetts, I experience a peculiar cycle of time as I once more clean the toilets, fold the sheets into the cedar chest, and vacuum the dust out of the summer house that Jonathan rents for his parents, whose health is failing. These are chores I have always hated and am not grateful to do again. Enlightenment.

In New York City, Bonnie cut her chorus practice because it was held on Mondays and I was in town and free on a Monday. Since then she and I have begun to talk on the phone, again, long distance, just as we did thirty years ago. Just as now I talk with Judith in Brockport, Sudie in Maine, Stephanie in Iowa, Sue in Idaho, Laura and Ayrie in Chicago, Charlotte in Vancouver. They have all come back, these dear old friends.

Enlightenment, loneliness, nostalgia, or love? I don't know. The voice I live with repeats, Breathe in *now!* Breathe in while I can, while the air is clear and the horizon still clean.

I wanted to see Washington, D.C., too, not in the eyes of a seventh-grader on a field trip, but as a political adult, a voter who has never taken *time* to sightsee in the city I read about every day. We sit in the Senate and watch our senator, Dianne Feinstein, battle a senator from Idaho over assault weapons. He calls her a "gentle lady." She tells him she is a woman whose political career was baptized in blood. I remember that blood. I was in San Francisco when the mayor, George Moscone, and a supervisor, Harvey Milk, were murdered by another supervisor, Dan White. I remember the day that Dianne became our mayor. We are not gentle ladies anymore.

At the Smithsonian, Jonathan spends an afternoon in the Aeronautics and Space Exhibit, while I attach myself to a carefully nonpartisan docent tour of the First Ladies' exhibit. From Martha through Hillary these women, also, were baptized in blood, sometimes in the back of a theater or an open-air limousine, sometimes by routine infidelities. With the notable exception of Jacqueline Kennedy, the press and public have demonstrated little interest in how these women finished their lives. Eighty percent of the obituary columns in the *San Francisco Chronicle* describe the lives of dead *men*. I know. I've been keeping track since 1991. Parentage is marked by paternity. A dead man is often the son of a father, rarely of a mother.

We visit the Vietnam War Memorial. I touch the names of boys I knew in high school and college. We cannot get into the Holocaust Museum, where now an uproar is had about the absence of Jewish women's deaths.

Jonathan's eighty-nine-year-old father dies while we are in Washington. We hear Rachmaninoff's Second Piano Concerto that night at the Kennedy Center. Will my children attend a concert in my memory? Will I have a paragraph on the obituary page?

"Take a picture of me," I instruct Jonathan. "Take a good one, for God's sake."

He doesn't. I have in mind a portrait. He catches me in candid poses.

"You *never* do what I say!" I yell. "You don't listen to me. I hate these damned pictures!"

"What's the matter with you?" he demands. "You don't like anything these days."

What I have neglected to tell him is that the portrait I have in mind will hang in the Jung Institute Library with the other deceased analysts. I forget to tell him that we are working on my obituary photo here.

Sometimes I tell him what he is meant to say at my funeral.

"I'm going to tell them," he responds, "that even when you were dying, you couldn't trust me to speak for myself."

Oh, such is the peace and tranquillity, the trust and acceptance, of enlightenment.

An obituary photograph is meant to show exactly who I was and what I looked like. But since cancer treatment, that image is a continually confusing one. I *do not know* what I look like. Once, when I was in treatment, and bald, we were driving through an intersection and I noticed that the driver approaching from the right had short, telling, chemo-curls. I snatched off my beefeater hat and waved at her. When she saw me she tooted the horn, gave me thumbs up, grinned. The woman in the passenger seat, older, more sedate (her mother, I fantasize), smiled tentatively. I felt giddily victorious. I knew what my battle was, then. I knew what I looked like. You couldn't keep us cancer folk down. We *knew* each other, goddamnit.

Now my status is not so clear. These days I experiment with haircuts and dye jobs. My old beefeater hat is stuffed into a basket in my closet. It is cold this winter, and the wind ruffles my baby-fine hair, but I cannot bring myself to wear that hat. My scarves lie beautiful and untouched in the bureau drawer. I will not even drape one over my shoulders. Whenever I see a woman with a scarf around her head, I check to see if she has eyebrows. Is the scarf for fashion or for chemo? Frequently I see a woman at my grocery store who has eyebrows drawn on her face. I know she is wearing a wig. I know she is in lifelong chemotherapy. Now, strangely removed from the immediacy of cancer *treatment,* I do not speak to her. Similarly, in a restaurant, I see a bold cancer patient with her bald head undisguised. I want to speak to her, but don't. I am not in treatment anymore. I no longer feel entitled to reach out to strangers with bald heads. Enlightenment does not seem to extend that far.

Months after the bone marrow transplant, when my hair was still radically short and I was still weak, my friend Chauncy took me for a slow walk. I took her arm as we crossed the six-lane intersection at Lombard and Broderick.

"Fucking dykes!" a carload of young blond heterosexuals, all female, yelled at us, proclaiming my return to the world of the healthy.

I look normal now. No one calls me names. Do I

miss it? Do I miss the camaraderie? The attention? The clear focus of my daily life? When I am at the Cancer Center, and see my compatriots still in the midst of their treatment, when I sense every fiber of their energy focused on surviving it, I feel ages apart. Certainly I am less focused. Certainly I have lost determination. My life continues willy-nilly. I have nothing to do with the fact that I am still alive. Can I surrender to life as I once surrendered to cancer treatment?

Time has lost its linear qualities. Every day makes a circle. Each season recalls the season before. At Easter 1994 I remember Easter 1993 and 1992. The little bunny vases are filled with forget-me-nots and pansies. We are eating lavender and turquoise hard-boiled eggs again. The image of 1993, when I sat frail on my deck to watch this faithful yearly promise, returns to me in 1994. I feel the presence now of the people who visited me then. I remember them dropping by to check on me while I was home alone and too weak to go up and down the stairs. I can feel the depletion and depression. I remember being unable to enjoy anything. And then, in 1993, just as in 1992 and 1994, the baseball season began. The Giants played well, beyond all hope and prediction. Deep down, below my gut, in the plate tectonics of my life, energy shifted away from the horrendous treatment I had chosen in order to stay alive. Depression, my depression, lifted.

Easter 1994: I have achieved another year—with

the same bunny vases of forget-me-nots and pansies, the spring, baseball. Opening day. Our first game. Our seats are even better than the 1993 ones. Jonathan and I sit in Section 17 on the exact trajectory of a throw from short to first, foul-ball territory. Our first game is a winner.

When we get home we find we have just missed a call from Ethan. "Guess where I've been today?" I ask when I call him back. We have a routine, Ethan and I. During nationally televised games, when the Giants are particularly good *or* particularly bad, we call each other. There is never a plan, but whoever picks up the phone doesn't say "hello" but just starts right in, watching the game together.

"Did you see that?" we begin, without introduction.

This is Easter 1994. Baseball has reincarnated itself, and I have hair. I do not worry about sitting out in the sun for three hours. I have just eaten a super dog and drunk a Coke. My elder son has telephoned me. The Giants will certainly do it this year. Hope, like spring, is everywhere.

"Guess where I've been today?" I ask my son.

A long silence, not typical of Ethan.

"What do you mean?" he asks, his voice guarded. I hear the caution only in retrospect. My head holds only images of baseball and a new spring.

"Guess where I've been?"

"The doctor?"

Oh, God, there it is again. Lurking just beneath the

surface of every silence. Our family is cursed with the knowledge of fate, of our vulnerability. We are cursed with enlightenment. On this spring day, in 1994, when my son assumes that I am going to give him more bad news, I do not know who is more enlightened—me, for reimmersing myself in life, or Ethan, for his constant wariness.

The Giants didn't make it in 1994. Fate conspired for a baseball strike. We have, all of us, lost our innocence.

On my last birthday, Jonathan gave me more and better presents than any I have ever given him. From the north, where innocence lives in pristine and frozen purity, comes a cyclone of old feelings. Embarrassment. Financial concern. Shame. Then, from the south, where life is muckier, enter the new feelings. Joy. Gluttony. Delight. Pleasure. They meet in our bedroom, causing a storm of ecstasy.

"You win, goddamnit!" I blow at him. "You gave me more presents than I have *ever* given you." My husband just laughs. Our thin Protestant austerity dissolves. The real gift, I have learned, is to receive when one cannot repay. On this birthday, Don and Valerie have bought us tickets to see *Forever Tango.* Jonathan and I come home from it and dance. I boss him around, telling him how to stamp, how to kick out from the knee. He makes an elaborate, clumsy show. When I dip backward, he drops me on my head.

A drop on the head is nothing. Joy in the midst of pain is everything. Transplant pain is with me every day:

bone pain, joint pain, foot pain, esophageal pain, headaches, earaches, jaw pain, edema pain, tooth pain, bruised shins, difficulty swallowing, difficulty eliminating, heart fibrillations, shortness of breath, fatigue, fatigue, fatigue. I wake at night wide-eyed with pain in my thigh. 911 pain. The next morning it subsides. My feet don't work, plain and simple. I'd give all my new clothes, all the CDs, the voice mail, and the new windows for a new spine. The ache between my shoulder blades makes me grouchy. I slump. My posture is atrocious. Swimming helps, I suppose, but sometimes I am so tired after a swim that I lie in bed for the rest of the day. I decide each night which pill to take. For sleep? Pain? Constipation? Dizziness? Nausea? I'm on 25 milligrams of digoxin for my chemo-weakened heart. If I don't rest, *every* day, I pay a price, a large one, far higher than the cost of all our remodeling and travel and a new Ford Ranger XLT. If I don't rest for two or three hours *every* afternoon, if I stay up past 8:30, I cannot function the next day. I cannot exercise. I cannot make dinner. I cannot play Scrabble. I cannot read. Enlightenment is worth none of this pain.

Jonathan, who reads a book every day, falls asleep without thinking. I sleep for ten minutes, wake, toss, fight hot flashes, turn on my new reading light and read the same novel I've been reading for weeks. The ache in my thigh returns. The blue meanies visit me in the night. I see my own funeral from above. I watch people take their places in the pews of an unknown church. I weep for their grief. "Let go," I tell myself. "You must let go." I must leave their grief to them.

I dreamed I won the MacArthur genius award. At the presentation, I was given a yellow gourd. The gourd came from a pumpkin seed in my compost pile. Pumpkin to jack-o'-lantern to compost to garden to pumpkin to gourd. Before enlightenment—chop wood, carry water, compost waste. After enlightenment—chop wood, carry water, compost waste.

The children seem more ready now. They don't seem to be struggling with daily tests of enlightenment anymore. Their readiness for me to die is demonstrated when Maggie tells me a dream of being born at twenty years of age. In the dream she is very tired. She has gone out with friends, but terrible fatigue brings her home. Then she sees me standing in the kitchen. I am much diminished in size, no longer larger than she is, and I am hugely pregnant. I tell her that her birth is imminent. Ethan appears and informs her that being born at age twenty is most unusual. I turn to her. "The time has come," I tell her. "You will be born today." Her fatigue evaporates and she brims with excitement, thrilling to be born.

James, in pursuit of an acting career, has become the main repairman for 16,000 Mac computers at the University of California at San Francisco, a skill that will assure him an income wherever he ends up. He rents the apartment below his father's house. Ethan and Nancy are happy. He tells me he wants to celebrate

Christmas with his children exactly as I did with him, before his father and I divorced.

About Jonathan, I am not so sure. The interweaving of our lives encircles every day we have. An echo of the good wife past, lifting her sleepy head, worries about him on his own, alone. She pesters him about how he'll handle money and frets that he will not be able, without my disability checks, to afford living in this house. She suggests to him, angrily, that he will retreat from social life, that he will fend off the sincere concern of our friends. The bad wife, the one he has now, leaves him alone. I leave him to figure out for himself how to manage when I die. He tells me that he's not interested in women anymore, that he'll never remarry. Old goody-two-shoes wife is afraid that this might be true. Me? I think life with me has been such a trial that he is just burned-out, exhausted, forever soured on the very idea of women. Jonathan's good wife, the one who never had cancer, doesn't think he'll eat right when she is no longer around to cook his meals. She worries that he will eat too many cookies and drink too much coffee and booze. Me? I make lemon squares, prune wheels, spice cookies, apple pie.

I stand above my husband as he lies in the bathtub reading and ask him, seriously, to commit suicide with me. I figure that as my disease wastes me, we could overdose together. The thought of separation is sometimes so intolerable that the idea of taking him with me, to the other side, is the only way to contemplate it.

Jonathan declines. Sitting in the bathtub, he looks me straight in the eye and says no. Really. Straight in the eye. No.

Let go the Ego.
Surrender to God.
Let him live—without me.

That is my late-night mantra.

Enlightened or not, newly spiritual or materialistic, my life, the same as it ever was, has changed. When I go for my biannual mammogram, I *forget* that all the women in *that* waiting room do not have cancer. So my comments comparing those magazines to the ones in Radiation Oncology are met with a shocked silence. Their eyes suddenly do not see me. Subtle shifts in their postures shoulder me away. Their attention flees from me as salt on the surface of oily water flees from pepper.

"Oh yeah, right," I realize, devil-laughter teasing the corners of my mouth, enticing me to feel superior and scornful. "These women live in the before," I remind myself. "They are still afraid of the *beginning*."

16

SEX, SHIT, MENOPAUSE, AND MONEY: THE SECRETS OF REMISSION

I YEARN FOR precancer days. Women without cancer appear to me as carefree and confident as the popular girls from high school who clustered around their lockers combing their hair and making an ado about clothes and makeup. I, just back in town, circle. I envy them, but I don't. Carefree as they appear, the popular girls seem naive and untested. What lives they seem to lead, with energy and muscle tone and glowing skin. I don't know if I would aspire again to laugh at dorks and nerds and girls who carry purses and get permanents. Did I ever really want to look down my nose at girls who didn't have boyfriends? A boyfriend was a ticket of admission our freshman year. I didn't make it. But how liberating it would be to try again. How luxurious to make a big deal of zits and greasy hair, a case of flu, a disk problem, an elevated cholesterol count.

Healthy women seem to think they will live forever. They know about death but it comes only to other people. They even like their bodies (though they pretend they don't), and we, whose bodies have been too tall, fat, dark, freckled, or poisoned, are weak with envy.

I want to pass for healthy again. I want to be a fifty-three-year-old woman bitching about a normal menopause and asking for advice on whether or not to use hormone replacement therapy. I want to have lunches to complain about husbands and children and the stress of working and writing and keeping house and raising children and making dinner every night of the year. I yearn for that blessed stress of having it all.

And I would kill for estrogen. I would kill to have some choice about the dry wrinkles on my face and the extra fifteen pounds tamoxifen has brought. I'd kill for a little estrogen cream up the old wazoo that would grease the wheels of my creaky sex life. Please, God, don't let those popular girls know how sere my sex life has become. The same estrogen that keeps them glowing in middle age would kill me.

In the bone marrow transplant group, we wail the loss of our libidos. In one session someone blurted out that she had about as much feeling in her clitoris as on the tip of her elbow.

"Elbowitis," Faith named the disease.

We laughed. But it was such a woeful laugh. A wist-
fulness whispered through the room like the nostalgia
of a summer evening. "It just isn't like it was before."

We nodded, all of us, straight and gay, old and
young. Summers past bedevil us. Memories tease us
with what we cannot have. The camaraderie helps. But
who would choose this soulful company in such an arid,
deathly place? Who would choose our postchemo
bonding over the old fears of dating, rejection, preg-
nancy, and STDs? Oh, I do miss regular, down-home
relationship stress: lack of sexual partners, birth control,
foreplay, difference in sexual appetites, failure in com-
mitment, even old-fashioned distaste as in, "Yes, I know
we get it on but I guess I just don't like you very much!"

I am in remission now, so there are days when I
pass for healthy. And because the world believes, as I
once believed, that remission means cure, I pass for
cancer-free, troubles behind me, cured, and in denial.
The increase in denial that remission brings feels nice.
It makes me strive to belong again. I am tired of being
"us," as a stricken friend puts it. I want to go back to
being "them." I want to laugh about ordinary, middle-
aged aches and pains, about the gray in my hair and the
wattle under my chin. I want to make plans for 1998 as
simply as I planned ahead in 1990. To my horror, I find
the self-assured and determined ideas healthy people have,
ideas about what it means to be sick—about *the right way*
to be sick—returning to me. A shiningly popular girl
gets whammied with cancer (or heart disease or lupus

or myasthenia gravis—there are other life-shortening illnesses) and I commit all the insensitive sins I railed against one short year ago.

"Oh, don't worry," I say. "The first chemo goes pretty quickly because you still have veins that work." It's kind of like hazing. "Well, I was on a heavy-duty chemo, one and a half times the strength of what you're going through." Keep your chin up, I am saying. It could be worse.

I give a lecture to a thoroughly disabled colleague. "Call Social Security," I tell her. "You've paid self-employment taxes all these years. Get an application for disability."

"Forms?" she asks.

"Right. It's a bureaucratic nightmare, but in the end you'll be approved and that $750 a month helps."

Her response is slow. "$750?" she asks. "I could get $750?"

"Right. Do it. Call them."

"All these things they expect you to be able to do when you can't think," she says. And then I remember. I remember that I could not balance my checkbook. I remember that I could not recall my mother's address. I remember Jonathan calling Social Security to provide the forms for me. Then I spent days fighting my befuddlement to create a self-employed profit-and-loss statement to resemble my twenty years of hard work as an independent practitioner. One of my dreads is that I will be held accountable one day for the figures I produced then.

But I give advice like this anyway. Stable now, and treatment-free, I regress into the bootstrap theory of serious illness. I give pep talks. I think of illness as something you get over, something to stop complaining about. I think to myself, "Oh, well, she doesn't have it so bad," which is really a way to establish that *no one* has had it as bad as I. My disease, no matter what someone else's is, is the standard from which I make all my pronouncements. I strut. Suddenly *my* hair is perfect, long again and straight. I have an arrogant twitch to my ass as I walk down the hall. I am waiting for the applause. I, and only I, will be the polio victim who learned to walk and became the homecoming queen, the thalidomide child elected class president. In my high school in the 1950s, anyone with a handicap was elected to class office and got a standing ovation at graduation. And all of us who voted for him or her were assured a place in heaven.

Then the nasty creature appears. I hear him rustling in the corner above the bookcase near my computer. He is waiting there, laughing. Half gargoyle, half leprechaun, and about four inches tall. In his hand is a list of my secrets, the embarrassing things I don't tell *anyone,* "us" or "them." Secrets that paint a mask over my face and fashion a passable smile.

"Oh, you are so smart, Mrs. Face-Up-to-Everything Cancer Queen," he smirks. "You think you've figured it all out!"

I don't want anything to do with him. I've told my story. There is nothing left unsaid. I am beyond shame, beyond embarrassment. I have catalogued every feeling of rage and despair. I have accepted my illness and my death. "You think!" he taunts.

He watches as Maggie, looking for a spare pair of pantyhose, finds my prosthesis where it lies, overnight and on days I don't leave the house, in my underwear drawer.

"Ohhh, Mom, I haven't seen this." She takes my flesh-colored silicone prosthesis out of the drawer and cups it in her hand. "This is weird," she tells me. My breast, the silicone one, wiggles through her fingers like Silly Putty. I do not like that. The breast adapts obscenely to her caress. I do not want to watch this. She should not play with my prosthesis.

"Put that back, Mags," I tell her with the same parental voice I used when she and Sophie were seven and eight and got into a box of Tampax. We know what it's for, I told them, now put it back.

Maggie, now age twenty, youthens to my tone. Her shoulders hunch under my reprimand. She is startled. So am I. Menstruation, mastectomy, bladder infections, birth control, safe sex—I thought we'd mastered these, mother to daughter. I thought I wore my breastlessness like a badge. Yet, in all this time, she has never seen my prosthesis.

Then my face threatens to go crumbly. Suddenly and still, after four years of trying to adapt to my amputation, I have not adjusted. Will I ever?

At my swim club, my prosthesis/breast slips out of my ugly, old-lady mastectomy bra and falls to the floor.

Embarrassment floods me like a hot flash. The prosthesis, out in the open, is far more embarrassing than the Amazonian scar across my chest.

The prosthesis is proof that I am trying to pass.

The Northern California Cancer Institute invites Jonathan to give a talk from the spouse's point of view at its second annual conference, "A Neglected Issue: The Sexual Side Effects of Breast Cancer Treatment." I missed the first conference because I was freshly out of the bone marrow unit and too weak to attend. I wanted to, though. Even then, even with that weakened shell of a body, I wanted my sex life back. I wanted to get home from the hospital, sick as I was, and reclaim my marriage bed. Sex and intimacy are affirmations of life, perhaps even more important in recovery than in the first blush of love. Perhaps as life-affirming in recovery as in conception.

At the conference on sexuality, I sit with Faith and her husband and listen to Jonathan talk to strangers about my body.

"The first revelation of breastlessness," he tells them, "the first look at the wound, is itself an intimacy, a trust and recovery. Rather like a first kiss. Likely, it's wordless, with much eye contact. Gesture is everything, a lingering caress, a kiss, perhaps shared tears."

I remember that moment, but I remember it differently. My chest was numb. I mean *numb*. Jonathan's head was ducked under my armpit somewhere, moving about. If he was caressing my scar, if he was kissing it lingeringly, I didn't know. What I knew was that his head was in the way and I couldn't feel anything.

"Then, in remarkably short order," he goes on describing his reaction, "nothing. Truly, *nothing* remarkable. How she looks is how she is, alive! Yum!"

Some partners, I hear, both hetero- and homosexual, leave when the breast goes. Some stay around and pretend nothing has happened. Their wives, in collusion, wear camisoles and prostheses to bed. Still others, like Jonathan, stay around and take on the whole life-changing event as though cancer had happened to them, which I suppose it has. At the conference, tears of recognition and envy surround me. I am one of the lucky ones. This is *my* husband speaking. He is telling these breast cancer patients and their partners about his reaction to a *New York Times Magazine* cover on which the artist Vronka had taken a picture of herself in a dress that revealed her mastectomy site.

"I looked at the photo as a fashion shot, assumed that—in the way of *haute couture*—someone had rediscovered Rudi Gernreich and 1960s high-fashion toplessness. It was only when, having messed up the crossword, I read the smarmy cover story that I even noticed Vronka's mastectomy."

That is what my husband said, in public, to hundreds of people sitting in a conference hall at the Hyatt Regency in San Francisco. Breastlessness has become, to Jonathan, commonplace. Having watched me undress for a thousand nights, he has come to think of all women as breastless. How nice—I think.

Granted, we do speak bravely of the emptiness of my bosom. Breastlessness is what the world seems to think breast cancer is about, after all. I can speak to that. But *I* am not ready to tell *anyone* that my libido has gone south, leaving a strange, powerful, but juiceless love in its place. Leave that task to Jonathan. When he stands there, at the podium, noting that I am alive, not dead, breastlessness is properly relegated to its place as a minor detail.

There is more, much more destruction wrought by breast cancer treatment than by mastectomy.

"The most direct thing this spouse can report to you," Jonathan informs what is now a rapt audience— he is about to impress them with our mind-boggling list of cancer therapies—"is that treating a premenopausal woman's Stage IV (*i.e.,* metastatic) breast cancer with radical mastectomy, a failed course of enhanced chemotherapy supported by an experimental white-cell colonizer protocol and follow-on radiation, to be followed by yet more radiation and two more courses of chemotherapy, then blood pheresis to collect peripheral stem cells, with a backup bone marrow harvest leading to autologous stem cell rescue (still popularly known as a bone marrow transplant) during a twenty-five-day hospital stay in semi-isolation . . . "

I am busy thinking to myself that he left out the unanesthetized surgeries when I hear the audience around me gasp. Jonathan hears it, too. He likes it, the show-off. Dramatically he looks up from his text and quips, "Got all that? It's the short list: it leaves out, for example, insertion of a foot-long triple-lumen vas-cath—it looked like a three-headed knitting needle—next to the previously installed sub-q Porta-Cath, which dealt with the collapsed-vein problem but which was useless in the stem cell rescue operation."

I'm getting a little squirmy here. The room is so quiet.

"The most direct thing I can report to you is that that entire process, completed for Christina and me almost exactly a year ago, has not been good for our sex life."

The audience, thank God, laughs. Finally there is some movement around me, some shoulders dropping, some reaching for Kleenex, some glances to friends and partners. No kidding, they laugh to each other.

"No kidding," Jonathan says.

I wish that all my fellow psychiatrists, psychologists, clinical social workers, marriage and family counselors, *and* Jungian analysts were sitting in this conference hall at this moment. I wish they were all here to take this bit of news in. Maybe then their endless suggestion that problems in sexuality following treatment for cancer have to do with *stress* and *problems within the relationship,* maybe that lofty, know-it-all, *wacko* idea would head south with my libido.

Couldn't you just kill them? All of them?

"If it has to do with problems with my husband," Faith asks, "then why aren't I checking out other men, the way I used to? Why aren't I looking around to see what other men are checking me out?!"

Amen.

I am not checking out other men. But I cannot, for the life of me, figure out why Jonathan is not checking out other women. Why isn't he ogling the popular girls, the ones who have entered menopause naturally, the ones who can take estrogen, or dong quai, or wild yam progesterone? Women whose vaginas are still moist and whose skin is free of the clammy slime of hot flashes. Women who will not mutter at him in the netherworld of sleep, "go 'way. I'm hot." Doesn't he want someone to cuddle with again, all night long? We used to do that. We used to sleep entwined like snakes on a sunny rock, perspiration-free. I used to drizzle my nipples across the hairs of his chest, too, and it used to turn me on.

The face of the nasty creature above my computer changes. In his role as keeper-of-the-secrets, he has many faces. For issues of sexuality, his taunting stops and his face goes blank as a robot. He will reveal nothing. The popular girls everywhere are going about their business. I am on the margins. To protect me, when he and I overhear the offhand sexual comments people make every day, the nasty creature makes his face inscrutable. Stoic. No one will guess from his expression that my libido is in the shop. We keep that secret.

Except in group. In group we wonder at all the ardent Hollywood couplings. Movies from *Basic Instinct* to *The Bridges of Madison County* strike us as about as interesting as a PBS *Nature* series. Clint Eastwood and Meryl Streep might as well be two praying mantises, for all the excitement they arouse. What a bizarre zoological habit this fuck business is.

Oh, it is so awful. Truly awful. And the worst part is that we get used to it. New group members ask us, "Does it get better?" "When will sex get back to normal again?"

We are gentle. Talk of increased intimacy through spirituality does not go over big at these times. "Well," we tell a plaintive woman who finished chemotherapy only six weeks ago, "there are some things you can do."

Back at the sexuality conference, Jonathan exclaims, "*Treatable!* Thank God or the pharmaceutical industry! Yes, the dryness and debriding friction is *treatable:* you all know the brand names: Replens, and Astro-Glide, and the old standby, K-Y jelly. In happy fact, for us K-Y jelly has become a kind of totem of good feeling and a stage of intimate progress: we keep ours in the drawer of the table on my side of the bed—it has become my love offering at the appropriate stage of our renewed and renewing, if much-changed and fragile, sexual intimacy."

A little exhibitionistic, perhaps, but the audience is still attentive. They need to hear this. They want to know and hardly anyone else has told them. Looking around at their attentive faces, I wonder how many of them have wondered, as I have wondered in retrospect, how we would have responded to the question no doctor posed. What would I have chosen, knowing then what I know now? What if the doctors had looked me straight in the eye when we were discussing how to blast the stealthy progression of cancer spreading from my breast to my lymph nodes to my spine and asked, "Which do you choose: your life or your easy sexuality? I can't give you both." I would have picked life. I know that. But I also know that I would not have believed him. As a Jungian analyst, I did not have the capacity to believe that anything *physical* could tamper with, let alone *destroy*, my sexuality.

Jonathan continues: "Yet appearance and vaginal dryness and renewal are nowhere near the half of it. One of cancer's most horrible sites for us was Christina's libido, once fertile, luxuriant, suggestive, and—not so many months ago, she told me in sad candor—*dead.* Not a sexual thought, not a lust, for months.

"Was that the low point for us? The nadir?

"How can I measure the relative depths of low point after low point after low point after low point?"

Oh, it was a horrible time. My head ducks into my chest. Such a horrible time.

"Just say *bad spot* and let it go at that," Jonathan braves his way. "*Bad spot* for us both, this loss of libido. Made me feel rejected, inept, or, worse and occasionally, like a wife abuser."

I remember that, too. I remember feeling as though he were a wife abuser. And I remember desperately vowing never to let him know. He knew anyway, just as a child knows, in his gut, that his parents are fighting when they say they aren't. Jonathan knew when I was just going along. Our secrets are out, I guess. I wanted him to go on wanting me, you see. If I couldn't feel my own passion, I could feel his. I needed him to carry enough passion for both of us. I also knew he'd never touch me if he thought he was hurting me. The nasty creature on my shoulder shudders. He gives a little tremulous sigh.

My eyes are on the table in front of me. I can't look around the room anymore. Jonathan's voice comes through the microphone, resonant and full: "But still, in the Faustian world of medicine that most of us here have signed in to," he tells our comrades, "*treatable.*" There *is* a test—it measures serum testosterone—and pills (they're called Halotestin or methyltestosterone)—and even a wan joke, 'So who takes the testosterone, you or me?'

"Get the blood test, check with your physician. If your testosterone count is low, this pill works. Wonderfully," he chuckles here and I see women digging in their purses for pens, madly scribbling on their notepads. I see their partners nudge them—did you get that? Write that down.

I did take testosterone for a while. I think the lower range of a normal woman's serum testosterone loiters around 30 (units of something or other). Mine was 4. I got the pill. It woke me up. The sappy lyrics to country-and-western ballads suddenly made sense again. I realized again why Michael Douglas and Clint Eastwood are considered attractive.

Yet testosterone doesn't do much for romance, I

discovered. It brings a heightened kind of jerk-off energy. But it helped me get started again. I don't take it anymore. Four months was about enough, but it pushed me over my hesitancies and embarrassments. It reintroduced my orgasmic confidence. It provided the bridge that chemotherapy had bombed out, the bridge between loving thoughts and bodily lust.

Also, taking testosterone helped me rebuild destroyed muscle, quickly. Life is so impossibly unfair that muscle development is much easier for the testosterone-laden. Jonathan took a photo of me at Sophie's high school graduation. I was sitting at a picnic table and laughing with her friends about how tight my butt was, simply from swimming twice a week. I was insisting that Sophie's friends feel my ass. I made her boyfriend feel it. Hard, tight ass. Testosterone ass. Jonathan took a picture. Just my face. The popular girls will never know to what lengths I went to achieve that expression.

But then they don't need testosterone. They don't need melatonin either, or stool softeners. They don't need to set aside half a day just to have a bowel movement. Elimination, that's another secret the nasty creature keeps. In the support group, Jay comes back from the bathroom and asks, "Can we talk shit here?" Yes. We can. Cancer support groups are the only place we can talk shit, for real. Black, bloody stools, we agree, are not good. Metastasis. Possibly colon cancer—metastasis or new primary? Possibly beets. Does Jay know about beets? Once, before cancer, I mistakenly went to the emergency room because I didn't know that beets show up red in the toilet. If we didn't talk shit in my bone marrow group, we wouldn't have been able to educate Jay about the beets and she would have suffered through yet another diagnostic test—this time an unpleasant, uncomfortable, and degrading sigmoidoscopy.

Blood or beet juice in the stools. Diarrhea. Constipation. Concrete stools so large that sometimes I think I have given birth through the wrong passage. Sometimes forceps are necessary. My plumbing is so scoured that it screeches when I use it. I keep having to use a wrench to get it started. This cannot be good for me. And certainly I do not want anyone to know. My doctor tells me to eat more fruit and fiber. I shake my head and say nothing. Fruit and fiber? Come on. For the disposal system I recommend daily Chinese herbs prescribed by a competent doctor of Chinese medicine.

In the old days, we never talked shit in front of the lockers, or at lunches when we complained about boyfriends and husbands. We didn't mention sleep much either, because we just did it. I mean normal women, as I recall, the ones I'll never really be one of again, just go to sleep when they get tired, don't they? My worst hot flash of the day is timed by the devil to occur exactly—Jonathan can verify this—eight minutes after I have fallen asleep, every night. Then its cousins come to visit every two hours, exactly, for the duration of my exhausting sleep. Hot flashes are not just sweaty events, as I assumed before I had one, but jazzed-up, caffeinelike, jittery prologues to a swampy, slimy soak. When I first had hot flashes I almost jumped out of bed with irritability. I think those estrogen-laden, noncancer women just go to bed and sleep eight or ten hours and then wake up feeling rested. Have I got that right? Does my memory serve correctly? I mean, I'm not idealizing anything here, am I?

The nasty creature is checking off the secrets, one by one. He taunts. He goes blank. He puts on a plastic face. And then he goes still and quiet. The rustling stops. He has come to the end of the list, to the very last and biggest secret of all. He has come to money. The list wafts out of his gnarly little hand and drifts to the computer desk where I can see every word. Just look at all the money secrets: income, job security, tenure, investments, health insurance, private disability, Social Security disability, and class. Between Jonathan and me, we had them all. Not so other Stage IV cancer patients. Sadly but truly not so.

I look at the list. The nasty creature has gone all bunny. He sits with his head on his paws, only his nose twitching. Please, God, don't let them notice me here in the brier patch. We have money, his little nose spells out. We have adequate health insurance. My husband is a tenured professor. When his health insurance refused to approve the bone marrow transplant, that $200,000 life extender that has provided this family three extra, treatment-free years, when his insurance company denied payment, my mother gave me $100,000. Because of Martha and Lynn, loving family and friends raised another $40,000.

Other women's cancer stories circle me like guilt, its pungent incense clouding the air. I know women who worked full-time during six months of chemotherapy and two more of radiation. I know women whose bosses cut them no slack when their hair was gone and their skin was gray. I know a woman too debilitated to return to work after chemo who lost her job and eventually her health insurance. One woman commuted to her job, an hour each way by train. Then she took two city buses to her downtown job as a legal secretary. She used the time on the train for throwing up. Five days a week she threw up down the jiggly, smelly commute-train toilet hole. Five days a week for six months.

On Fridays the chemotherapy wards and oncology offices are crowded. The IV bags resemble a conference of jellyfish as they hang every which way, swaying in the jostle as nurses and technicians rush to infuse cancer chemicals into patients who have to be back at work the following Monday. I never had to do that. I took my chemo on a Monday and spent the next week in bed, my bed, in my home, which I own. Friends came by every day to check on me. And my telephone rang. And messages were left on my machine. And people sent me letters and cards and flowers and books and tapes. A colleague arranged for Jung Institute members to contribute money for food to be delivered, month after month.

I know a single mother who was twenty-nine at the time of her bone marrow transplant. She says she didn't get any casseroles except when her mother made one. Now she is back at work full-time, struggling with about $50 per month in discretionary income. She chooses cable TV.

"I know I should be saving," she says, "but it's what we like best on a Saturday night: pizza and Nickelodeon."

What if someone discovers I bought Jonathan a pickup truck in *cash?* In the summer of 1994, a year and a half after transplant, when I turned out to be alive, I maneuvered our medical funds to find enough money for it. He still shakes his head and whistles when he realizes we are not paying off a car loan. I used the money we had earmarked to pay off medical bills, rationalizing that hospitals do not charge interest on monthly payments, while car sharks do.

I have not become so blasé that I don't worry what people will think of me for this behavior. I don't like the impression our apparent riches might leave in the minds of devoted friends who contributed to the Christina Middlebrook Bone Marrow Fund. Will they think I took the money and squandered it? Will they think the whole fund was a hoax? I don't like it when Jonathan tells friends that "Christina bought me a truck." I don't want a hospital bill collector to appear on my doorstep with the results of a means test, proving that I could have paid them first.

The bunny inside me practically shrivels. We have

been so lucky. I never put off a medical appointment I want in order to save money. I never decline a bone scan or an MRI or MUGA or CT or lab work for financial reasons. And I've added other expenses too, the extras that a lean and mean new health system will deny most people—treatments like Jungian analysis and cancer support groups and massage and acupuncture. Maybe, if there are T or TN antigens bound to my tumor cells, I will begin a commute to Chicago for a trial vaccine. We have the means to figure out a way to do that.

So many of my fellow metastatic cancer patient friends who soldiered through a world that did not want to know what was going on with them are dead now. The others who are living still cannot afford to be bunnies. They have had to develop hard and burdensome shells. They are tortoises, now, stumbling and slow. I have been able to keep my tender skin. I have been able to go at my own pace. Money, expenses, bills, debts, credit, disability payments—I have them all. And though I move money around like peas under walnut shells, I have the peas. I have the walnut shells.

I never thought I'd say this. Shoot me for saying it. It is one of those things that "they" say—those healthy, popular, normal people. But this is one of my secrets too. I have been very lucky.

17
THE DIER

———————— ❧ ————————

M Y SON Ethan, now in his fourth year of medical school, is steeped in science and his heart
is fixed on curing. He wants to make children's lives better. He complains to me, "Psychiatrists
don't know their medicine." When he tells me this, he
means to be critical. He scowls.

But, much as I love him, I can shrug off my son's
implied criticism of my chosen field. "Why should
they?" I think, defending psychiatrists. "Why should
they know their medicine?" I practice psychotherapy
under a clinical social work license and have been a
Jungian analyst since 1985. If you were to ask me today
the questions we tossed around in graduate school—Is
psychiatry art or science? Is it religion or logic?—I
would have little hesitation answering. "Art," I would
respond. "Religion," though I hardly mean the dogma
of the religions that attract people into churches and
synagogues.

I am not talking about the Christian Coalition here. I am talking about the difference between Ego and Psyche. I am referring to how, once a person has sorted out all his family stuff—the inevitable unmet needs and unresolved dependencies, the enviousness, competitions, anger, and guilt—the autonomous reality of the Psyche appears. Life, and its partner, death, belong to the Psyche, that infinite, unknowable cosmic order that human beings can neither know nor control. In Jung's theory, that distinction, the one between Ego and Psyche, is what has sustained me in my struggle to accept an early death. My death will come in its natural way, in its own time, even if that time is not of the Ego's choosing. The Psyche holds a force of life that is not controlled by willpower and is far larger than what the Ego can know.

This answer I have found, about art and science, religion and logic, comes from the experience of having handed my body, all of it, without reservation or compromise, over to medicine in order to prolong my life. Medical science has kept my Stage IV cancer stable for three and a half years, and in that process has, occasionally, shown a wanton disregard for the quality of my life. While radiating my L-2 and T-5 vertebrae, my radiation oncologist handled my complaints of esophageal pain by prescribing a pint of Tylenol with codeine as well as a vial of liquid Xylocaine. He never once made a physical exam.

Fortunately my surgeon, less engrossed in technology (therefore earning half the income of the radiation oncologist), had a different approach. She remembered that I was a person.

"Open your mouth," she said. "Let me see." Pause, tongue depresser, gag. "You have a wicked case of thrush!"

Then she wrote a prescription for mycelex troches that would actually treat my yeast-infested throat rather than just dulling my pain. The radiation oncologist hardly reacted when I informed him of his misdiagnosis. He was too busy looking at my films and calibrating radiation doses. My surgeon has retained the art of medicine. My radiation oncologist is lost to its science.

Medicine and high technology have not been adequate to the task of teaching me how to live, daily, with this disease. In no way has either helped me prepare for death. Medicine and technology are twins born of logic, and logic belongs to the Ego.

"You are not thinking right," my mother told me when, during the year after the transplant (a time period when 50 percent of Stage IV patients have a recurrence), I declined to have more tests to measure the progression or stability of my disease. She mistook this to mean that I had given up. Now, my mother and I simply do not talk about cancer or its treatments or the treatment side effects. Finally, it has occurred to me that her avoidance comes from loving me and not wanting me to die before she does. About her own death, she quotes Woody Allen: "You know what they say—I'm not afraid of death, I just don't want to be there when it happens." She does not want to be there while mine happens, either. My brother telephones and visits much more frequently than he used to, which I love, but he still waits until I am out of the room to ask Jonathan how I am doing. And, recently, a friend asked Jonathan if I had been able to put the bone marrow transplant experience behind me. She appeared to believe that not thinking about my body's suffering would help me return to normal life.

"Well, we're not going to pretend it never happened," Jonathan said. When he repeated the conversation to me, I wondered why recovering from cancer treatment and living with cancer do not count as normal life.

By contrast to those who choose to turn away from the darkness of terminal illness, a Jungian colleague who faced a lesser breast cancer remarked, "I just don't want to forget that this has happened to me." Perhaps we are in a minority, but this seems to be our way. We struggle to accept every event of our lives. We are zealous believers in integration and vehement enemies of repression.

Facing the end of my life earlier than I had expected, I am determined to make analytic psychology and terminal illness meld, so that one is not sealed off in a compartment from the other. Because of my Jungian orientation, people keep expecting me to *know* something about facing this ordeal. The expectation is that my education will have provided me with a special understanding about my personal life as I face death. Perhaps it has. But I dislike theories and, most of all, the jargon and categories that bury meaning alive. Intellectual understanding pales before experience. What I know is that I don't know. Analytic psychology gives me the equipment I need to face not knowing: "One does not become enlightened by imagining figures of light, but by making the darkness conscious" (Jung).

The children's friends are at an age now, their middle twenties, when they are suddenly aware that I am something other than a mother, that I have a profession. My sons were at the end of their college years before they even set foot in the C. G. Jung Institute of San Francisco, and those first steps were to attend a Christmas party.

"What does my mom do here?" they asked my colleagues. Unable to get a succinct answer from anyone, they concluded that my whole association there was an elaborate ruse. I am delighted that I have left them free for their own discoveries. Leah, who has a great interest in psychoanalytic criticism, has never asked me a single question about Jung. This is fine with me.

"I think of all the times I've been in your house," said a friend of Ethan's, who is studying for a master's degree in marriage, family, and child counseling, "and we never talk about your work."

"Well," I tell Ethan's friend. "I'm not big on talking about it. I'd rather just live it. The main idea of my work is that each individual needs to find his own way."

One can never really describe the depth of an analytic experience. It defies rational translation. The jargon and labels and theories that evolve are inadequate to convey what actually goes on in transference and regression, or to describe the vibrant healing power of symbolic transformation. Jo Wheelwright, an early mentor of mine, tells how he would leave the room whenever his fellow psychiatrists began to discuss diagnoses. Of course, I do know my diagnoses—as in any professional language, psychological terms are useful—but I rarely think of them while I am working.

Nevertheless, when the shit hit the fan, when they told me I might be dead in two years, I turned every stone to find any theory, any piece of jargon, any promise of a mind-over-body cure. I searched my dreams looking for any clue to my prognosis. All my positive interpretations were wrong. In that shocking month of August 1991, I clung to my dreams as though they were fortune tellers. I dreamed of a great system of canals and locks that had been scoured clean. I thought that meant no lymph node involvement. Now I think my psyche was preparing for chemotherapy. I reduced my dreams to simple predictions, much as once, after a painful breakup with a lover, I read the daily horoscopes in the newspaper. Fear had reduced me to wishful thinking. But dreams are not part of a how-to manual. They come from the gigantic scope of the Psyche and don't concern themselves with petty predictions.

My understanding of dreams and my belief in what Jung has discovered about the reality of the Psyche have been put to the test these cancer years. Before cancer, Jung's explication of the collective unconscious, his discovery that images extend from one culture to another, from one century to another, informed my life. The idea that my journey through life might be a meaningful part of a meaningful whole was simultaneously soothing and inspiring.

Often I dream of a lost or scorned child. This archetypal symbol enlarges to include not only the Christ child but also Quetzalcoatl, or Moses, or the promise of any new life potentially threatened. Likewise images of reincarnation, of alchemical change, of foolishness and wisdom, beauty and evil—all expanded with meaning when I studied them in the light of art history, literature, religion, anthropology. For an example from pre-cancer days, I remember how relieved I was, after discovering the Brontë sisters, when I clearly understood how, throughout all culture and all time, one gender has projected its soul upon the other.

Since cancer, I have had to figure out how my reality, enormous to me but small in the realm of all nature, fits into the archetypal reality I just described. Facing a terminal illness, I wonder how much Jungian theory is mere speculation. Is it, perhaps, a mere egocentric construction to defend against hopelessness? Could it be a technique for deflecting the blunt harshness of life? I have asked myself how much my own cataloguing of symbols comes from reluctance to face the unadorned ugliness of suffering. How much does my embracing of the symbol—of battle or victory, of hero or martyr—serve to camouflage the tininess of my own life? I have discovered, without a doubt, that to make real the archetypes Jung writes of, the symbols he cherishes, the metaphors and similes that inspire analytic work, one must move them out of the intellectual realm and embody them in actual experience. Thinking that an experience, advancement in a profession perhaps, is a life or death experience, is not the same as having a test for HIV or awaiting the results of a biopsy.

I tried, in the beginning, to achieve the mind-over-body miracle. I read *Quantum Healing,* and *Love, Medicine, and Miracles.* I really tried to follow the advice of the Simontons and visualize Pac-man, that '70s cartoon scavenger, racing through my body chomping on bad cancer cells. Nothing. I couldn't count sheep, either, when I was younger. In my attempts to get to sleep, the sheep did not jump uniformly over a fence but muddled up in a pile. Equally muddled was Pac-man, whose journey through my body kept getting mired in my elbow. I didn't know where cancer was, so I didn't know where Pac-man should chomp. I'm good at meditating, fine at relaxing, but no good at all producing an inner cartoon of someone else's making.

The whole exercise made me feel inadequate, worried, and guilty. Was I furthering my disease by bad thoughts? Some would say yes. Each time I read of the miracles wrought by visualizing, I would wonder, "But what about metastasis? What about Stage IV? Were any of your miracle subjects already in Stage IV?" Then I'd experience that horrid fear that I was fueling cancer cells rather than destroying them. I did not need a fantastical worry added to a pile of actual, day-to-day, in-your-face traumas.

Eventually I understood the gimmick. The word *healing,* as used by Simonton and LeShan and Bernie Siegel, does not refer to a cure, which is what I wanted, but to an attitude to accompany me so that I can smile my way through this vile disease. I think dying is difficult enough without having to achieve a pleasant attitude in the process.

Bernie Siegel suggests that the cause of our cancers can be discovered by reviewing the particular stress we were under six to nine months before diagnosis. I spent a little time investigating that premise, too. The truth is that there was no time in the past decade in which I was not under some form of stress. I was raising children, working, divorcing, fretting about money, struggling with guilts and inferiorities, remarrying, stepparenting, studying, passing exams. These stresses do not differentiate me from other latter-twentieth-century women. Cancer does.

Besides, how can one determine the starting point of a cancer, that point at which the destructive stress can be discovered? Cancer can wait, undetected, in the body for *years* before it is discovered. If we were to follow Siegel's formula, we would have to build a theory around why some of us have enjoyed an early detection while others of us, sinners I guess, have suffered one that is too late. Is it my fault that my breast tissue was youthfully dense, making the mammograms obscure?

New Age tyranny suggests that if I have cancer I must have "needed" it in order to resolve some previous life issue that lies rotting beneath the surface of my life. Thus, because I got cancer in my breast, I must have been too maternal, or maybe not maternal enough. God save us all!

The implication that one's cancerous tumor is indicative of failure offends me down to my toes. The idea that death comes to those who deserve it is a cruel jibe by the currently healthy. Certainly death is a miserable outcome. Giving up life is horrible. No one wants to die. No one wants a loved one to die. Nevertheless, we all die. Each and every one of us. To insist that one will not die because of a superior lifestyle or a favored position in the eye of God seems unconscionably arrogant. My determination is to face what is coming, not to change it. I cannot overcome the unarguable fact that metastatic cancer is inevitably fatal.

In a 1956 letter to his cousin Rudolph, Jung wrote: "I have seen cases where the carcinoma broke out when a person comes to a halt at some essential point in his individuation or cannot get over an obstacle. . . . [Then] an inner process of growth must begin, and if this spontaneous creative activity is not performed by nature herself, the outcome can only be fatal."

Is Jung suggesting here that carcinoma progresses because of an obstacle in the Ego or Psyche? If one cannot distinguish between Ego and Psyche, one is going to misunderstand Jung's words, as I am afraid many have. Jung, different from New Agers, is speaking of the force of the unconscious, not of conscious will-power. Were he suggesting, which I do not believe he is, that there is an attitude we humans can assume that will prove to be a greater force than destiny, a greater power than God, or the Self, well, then, he and I would have had to part company.

Human beings put thousands of obstacles in the way of the Psyche. That obstruction is a sometimes necessary role of the Ego, which must function in a mundane world. The life struggle for everyone in the second half of life is to let go the Ego. For us cancer patients, that task just comes a little sooner. Some of us have skipped a generation or two. I, at fifty-three, speak comfortably about my body's decline with eighty-year-olds. Thirty-year-old women in my bone marrow trans-plant group, a group where I am decades older than most other members, turn to my generation to discuss their enforced menopause. Our letting go of the Ego comes early in the natural order of things. But we are not people who have failed. Women who are hit with virulent breast cancer in their premenopausal years have not done something wrong.

So where does the inner process of growth that Jung says must begin come from? From nature herself, from the same nonhuman place as death and life, which is to say, from the Psyche. I am not writing *nonhuman* here to mean *inhuman,* as in cold and sterile. I mean *nonhuman* as in large, unknowable, beyond the ken of our limited human understanding.

A very long time ago, after the discovery of my virulent, invasive, 2- to 3-centimeter tumor, already metastasized to my lymph nodes, already in my vertebrae, back in what seems a lifetime ago, when a friend spoke to me of "an enlightened death," I was offended.

"I am not interested in an enlightened death," I told him. "I'm interested in an enlightened life." But that was in the beginning, before the beaches and the jungle and the arid desert. The battle has changed me. Now, not only do I consider an enlightened death; I cannot imagine an enlightened life without including thoughts of an enlightened death. How could I have considered one without the other?

My ego fights this. My ego holds as tenaciously to life as anyone else's. I cannot imagine this world without me in it, or at least I couldn't in the beginning. There is nothing I, or any soldier or doctor or commander-in-chief, any director of hematology oncology or the Nobel Prize winner who discovered the oncogene, can do to change how bad I feel about dying in my fifties. My only ally is surrender. I find great relief in surrender. Surrender means I can stop worrying and fretting and figuring out what I am supposed to do. I can forget about beating odds and just live my life. I don't need to work harder than I already have, I tell myself, because I have already done everything that I can *and* because I didn't do anything wrong in the first place.

Last year, in the transplant unit, I had decided I was going to *have* to die. I did not choose death. I just thought it was coming to me. I thought it was my karma. My time. At night, approaching sleep, I admonished myself to let go, to die if that was what happened. In the morning, when my fungus-infested eyes were glued shut and I needed my fingers to pry them open, I would wake in the netherland, awake and unable to see. I was still alive, for one more day, one more fight, one more battle, one more stretch of pain, boredom, and vomiting. I would live one more day of fear, and adrenaline, and confusion, and worry, and love.

"Thank you for one more day," I found myself saying. I promised to say that to myself every morning for the rest of my life. I have recovered so far, now, as to fail that promise.

Sometimes it seems to me that, having already come so close to death, I am going to have to die twice. Having survived Fredericksburg, I find myself lined up for Pickett's charge. Here I am again in the language of war. Perhaps Joshua Chamberlain's weary troops at Gettysburg would dismiss my metaphor. "After all," they might rightly say, "no one in that transplant unit was trying to kill you. They were trying to save your life." This is true.

Just as real violence must be distinguished from televised violence and roadrunner crackups distinguished from helmetless motorcycle crashes, so must *symbolic* war, the story wars we see in movies or read about in books, and *symbolic* cancer, so frequently metaphorized, as in a "cancer on the presidency"—so must they all be distinguished from reality, from real violence, real war, and real cancer. Real cancer is not a metaphor.

War is war. Cancer is cancer. Symbolic death is not death. War, cancer, and death are archetypally real. The urge to soften them, to fend off their reality, to metaphorize them, this urge overpowers our ability to speak the truth. Our inability to speak these truths raw, to view them unadorned and plain, does not surprise me. Unmetaphorized war, cancer, and death are stark and terrifying.

The physical experience I had in the bone marrow transplant unit was not a metaphoric death. It was damned near a real one. As close as it came, however, it was not death.

"Death is brutal," wrote Jung, describing indiscriminate force as it strikes, randomly downing the vital and sparing worthless good-for-nothings: "a human being is torn away from us, and what remains is the icy stillness of death."

Jung wrote these words about death from the point of view of the Ego, which, of course, looks at death from the point of view of the one who is left behind. The dead cannot tell their story. We have so much more experience surviving the death of a loved one than we have of dying. When I was first diagnosed, I thought of death this way, from the aspect of the survivor, from the feelings of the person who attends the funeral. Ego, knowing that I would not be at my funeral, submerged itself in the grief of my survivors, my husband, children, and friends. Their grief was intolerable to me, identified as I still was with the people who continue to live. Loss, grief, rage, and abandonment are what grief-stricken egos know of death. I've come to understand, however, that though this may be how death appears to the ego of the survivor, it is not how death appears to the psyche of the *dier*.

I thought I made up this word. *Webster's Third* defines *dier* as "one who dies." The dictionary makes no elaboration. I do not find the word *dier* in that growing library of writings about cancer called "survivor stories," which I have combed for three years. Intelligent religious thinkers speak of the "lost," the "departed," and those who have "passed on." James Joyce writes "beastly dead," and Joseph Heller calls them "garbage." I like "dier."

There *is* a tiny library of books, not so popular, written by a few who write about the journey, shaped by cancer, from life through death. These I read avidly. *Cancer in Two Voices* by Barbara Rosenblum and Sandra

Butler. *Grace and Grit* by Kenneth and Treya Killam Wilbur. *Diary of a Zen Nun* by Nan Shin. These books are my treasures. These books are written by people who knew they were dying.

Barbara Rosenblum writes, ten months before she dies, and I love her for it: "If you think standing by yourself waiting for someone to talk to you is lonely, if you think holidays alone are lonely, if you think that not having a relationship for a long time is lonely, if you think that the long, frightening nights after a divorce are lonely—you cannot know the aloneness of one who faces death, looking it squarely in the eye."

Nan Shin, who died of ovarian cancer, is an American Zen nun who kept a diary of "every day living" during the time she was in chemotherapy. She begins her last published entry: "[D]oes this Zen and all this harmony-with-nature stuff enable one to deal any better with those times when long, close and enforced contact with a person, persons or situations bruises every sensibility, flays every nerve ending, assaults the intelligence, bores the mind to blindness, thwarts the heart and imprisons the body? Yes."

At the end of her book, when her death is imminent, Treya Wilbur murmurs to her husband, who, because he was not a dier, can report it, "Sweetie, I think it's time to go."

The women whose books I admire and whom I have just quoted were able to speak quite matter-of-factly of their approaching deaths, which is not to say without fear, anxiety, anger, and grief. None hid from the vision of her own lifelessness. I think it no coincidence that each was engaged in spiritual practice. Kenneth and Treya Wilbur bring a full compendium of mystical, Eastern, Western, Zen, Christian, transpersonal psychology to her five years of living with and then dying from cancer. Barbara Rosenblum reconnected with Judaism. Nan Shin was a fully practicing Zen Buddhist nun. Each, in her illness, succeeded, I think, in transcending the Ego.

The Ego's hold on the taboo that forbids us to speak of death, I have learned, is its strongest hold, stronger even than its censure of those other unmentionables: sex, money, incest, voting Democratic in the 1990s. Almost automatic words come out of our mouths to protect us from the reality of death when someone says she is dying.

"No you aren't," we protest.

"Don't talk that way!"

"Just think how lucky you are to _____." Fill in the blank—have a family, live near a good hospital, have lived thus far. The insistence on luckiness, I find, comes most frequently from older, healthy people.

Then there is, "You never know." I have struggled to find a response to "you never know." All I have come up with is "but, I do know," and that one makes me feel rude.

When I talked about my bone marrow transplant with an old boyfriend at a high school reunion (granted, maybe not the best place), he said, "You do seem edgy."

Edgy! Maybe I should learn to shut up. Truth be known, when I speak the words aloud—"I am dying" or "I will die of cancer"—if I mention my odds, mention that I am putting my house in order, mention sorting through papers, sorting through clothes, sorting through stuff, any of these neverending preparations that I take on with the energy that remission brings, I feel brazen. Or sometimes ashamed. Or, more ironically, I worry that if, after speaking these words and breaking the taboo, I do *not* die within the foreseeable future, if I surpass the three event-free years I am shooting for, I worry that I will be criticized for calling so much attention to myself.

Death is brutal. T. S. Eliot writes that "Human beings cannot stand much reality."

But, "[f]rom another point of view," Jung writes, referring to the point of view of the Psyche, "death appears as a joyful event. In the light of eternity, it is a wedding, a *mysterium coniunctionis*. The soul attains, as it were, its missing half. It achieves wholeness."

I do resonate to that last line: "The soul attains, as it were, its missing half. It achieves wholeness." How can the soul attain *wholeness,* that cosmic order we all seek, without including death? But does this make death a joyous event? Can't death's magnitude stand on its own without being interpreted in light of worldly events? "On Greek sarcophagi the joyous element was represented by dancing girls, on Etruscan tombs by banquets. When the pious Cabbalist Rabbi Simon ben Jochai came to die, his friends said that he was celebrating his wedding. To this day it is the custom in many regions to hold a picnic on the graves on All Souls' Day. Such customs express the feeling that death is really a festive occasion."

As much as I have come to accept death as a natural aspect of life, I think it demeans death's power to whitewash it with the words *festive* or *joyous*. It demeans my power to write as honestly as I have about my own death. I'm cross with Jung for suggesting these words. I think he is romanticizing ancient culture. In fact, I wonder if the followers of Rabbi Simon ben Jochai were not unlike present-day positive thinkers. The rabbi was not dying, they said. He was celebrating his wedding. I don't know why we should assume that human egos in ancient cultures were any less tenacious than our own. It's nice to think they weren't, that these peoples were more enlightened and feared death less than we do, but I don't think so. Humankind has always been humankind.

For my part, I wonder whether Rabbi Simon ben Jochai did not say to his friends, as I have said to mine, that he was not celebrating his wedding, but that he was dying. I wonder whether he did not wish, as I have wished, to de-metaphorize his life journey, which includes death. To do so, perhaps, would have made room for more than his ego and included his soul.

Recently an old friend came to visit. Barbara is someone who has not needed to deny the severity of my illness. She no longer lives in San Francisco but was passing through and wanted to spend some time together while I have time to spend. She had just suffered a death in her own family, which may be one of the reasons she is able to look at my prognosis so clearly. We talked about her loss, her survivorship. She was grieving that perhaps she had not spoken directly enough to her sister, whom she so loved and who was dying. I asked her what she wished she had said.

"I would have wanted to say, 'This is life's biggest transition. Go for it.'"

As our brief visit ended, she asked how we might keep in touch were I to become ill and out of communication again. She most specifically wanted to hear when my health once again declined.

"I just don't want to hear that you have already died," she told me.

I asked her why.

"So that I can write to you, to speak to you one last time."

"What would you say?"

"I'd want to tell you to *go for it*."

I think that's better than dancing girls on the sarcophagi, better than a wedding or festivity; better to have a witness who says, when the time comes, "This is life's biggest transition. Go for it."

❧   ❧   ❧

Ricki died on Tuesday. In the two weeks preceding, there was a flurry of activity, at her request, in the cancer support community. A fax campaign was launched to flood Genentech with requests to release their experimental HER2/NEU antibody to Ricki's doctor for compassionate use. I never got around to sending my fax, and I feel bad about that. I thought it was right for her to go on trying to live until she died.

However, I did spend some time with her. She did not live close by, but we were able to have two long conversations by telephone in the week before she died. She had declined more chemotherapy, in hopes, she told me, of having some quality time at the end of her life. That quality time was not materializing.

"I didn't know it would be this fast," Ricki said in our last conversation.

"How is that for you, dearheart?"

"It's a hard idea to get used to."

We made plans for me to visit, but I knew I would never see her again.

"Ricki," I made myself say, "you were the first person to have told me that death was not the worst thing in the world."

"I was?"

"Yes. You said that having watched the other members of your old support group die, you learned dying wasn't as bad as you had feared."

"Oh, the women in that group were a powerful bunch. I've never met such a group of women."

"You're like that for me. You told me they taught you that you'd be able to manage it, too."

"As if I had a choice!"

We laughed. "Thank you, sweetie," she said. "I'm glad something I said was helpful to you."

She died three days later.

The night I heard that Ricki had died, Maggie and I were lying together on my bed. Everybody else was out of town. It was just the two of us. With considerable ambivalence (how much of my death work should I lay on a twenty-year-old?), I decided to tell my daughter about Ricki.

"My friend Ricki died yesterday," I said.

She lifted her head from my arm and looked at me.

I told her about my last conversations with Ricki, about how Ricki had suggested to me that dying was not the worst thing in the world.

"Are you more ready now, for me to die?" I ask my daughter. "More ready than before?"

She is very still. During my illness she has grown from sixteen to twenty, and she has not forgotten the conversation we had after she failed her driver's test. I know she'll speak.

"*Ready*," she says, finally, "is an inhuman word. Let's say I'm more familiar with the idea."

We cry.

"What I figure is this," I tell her. "That I am going to live my life as richly as I can. If I don't die soon, what will I have lost?"

She nods.

Bless her, bless all my children, my husband, and my friends who have found the strength to stay with me in this journey. Bless them for not turning their pain of losing me into frantic activity to keep me alive, for not abandoning me by clinging to the illusive idea of keeping me with them.

So hold my hand. Love me. Weep with me our tears of separation. Release me to the inevitable. I am not imagining figures of light. I am making the darkness conscious.